# Sh*t
# Politicians
# *say*

# Sh*t
# Politicians *say*

**THE FUNNIEST, DUMBEST, MOST OUTRAGEOUS
THINGS EVER UTTERED BY OUR "LEADERS"**

WRITTEN AND COMPILED BY

**JESSE VENTURA**

Skyhorse Publishing

Skyhorse Publishing books may be purchased in bulk at special discounts for sales promotion, corporate gifts, fund-raising, or educational purposes. Special editions can also be created to specifications. For details, contact the Special Sales Department, Skyhorse Publishing, 307 West 36th Street, 11th Floor, New York, NY 10018 or info@skyhorsepublishing.com.

Skyhorse® and Skyhorse Publishing® are registered trademarks of Skyhorse Publishing, Inc.®, a Delaware corporation.

Visit our website at www.skyhorsepublishing.com.

10 9 8 7 6 5 4 3 2 1

Library of Congress Cataloging-in-Publication Data is available on file.

Cover design by Brian Peterson
Cover photo and interior photos credit: AP images

Print ISBN: 978-1-5107-1417-5
Ebook ISBN: 978-1-5107-1418-2

Printed in the United States of America

# Dedication

*I want to dedicate this book to my father and mother...*

*To my father George—sergeant, World War II veteran, recipient of six Bronze Battle Stars, who, at the dinner table, frequently referred to Nixon as "the tailless rat."*

*And to my mother, Bernice—lieutenant, World War II veteran, nurse, served in North Africa. She always had the courage to send George to the basement when he got too wound up.*

# Acknowledgments

To the folks at Skyhorse—thanks for your diligent work. Special thanks to Joe Craig, Stacey Fischkelta, Jacob Klein, Mike Lewis, Jill Lichtenstadter, Rachel Mongomery, Brian Peterson, Steven Sussman, and Bill Wolfsthal. And special appreciation to Tony Lyons, for the courage he shows whenever he publishes me.

# *Table of Contents*

# *Introduction*

"In America, you have a right to be stupid, if you want to be. And you have a right to be disconnected to somebody else if you want to be. And we tolerate that—we somehow make it through that."

—John Kerry, in his first trip overseas
as secretary of state, 2013

"The American people have grown stupid, we've grown uninterested, we've gotten busy, we're distracted, we're lazy, and we're easily manipulated. Again, I can sit with you and have a beer and I can tell you about how idiotic most of our politicians are. That's boring to me. It's on us. Jefferson said something to the effect of, when a people becomes uninformed or uneducated—stupid—they're going to lose their republic, they're going to lose this democracy. And folks, I'm here to tell ya with a big old smile, we're there. We're losing."

—Joe Walsh (IL) at a town hall
meeting in 2013

In the words of Bob Dole, "If you're hanging around with nothing to do and the zoo is closed, come over to the Senate. You'll get the same kind of feeling and you won't have to pay." Since the dawn of politics, leaders and leader wannabes have opened their mouths, letting the stupid loose from their brains. We've watched the people running our countries closely for centuries, and we've heard just about everything, ranging from gaffes, rude remarks, and boorishness, to nastiness and malicious targeting.

While the Greeks and Romans had formal government in their day, it wasn't until after the American and French Revolutions that we could vote our stupid leaders back in office, rather than just have them be born into a stupid, royal family. And since we have the freedom of speech to criticize them, as well as the right to vote for them, I wrote this book.

When I sat down for my interview in *Playboy* magazine back in 1999, I called out a lot of bullshit. From religion, to inept leaders, to fat people—I was honest. And I got a lot of shit for it. And even though people called me stupid, today I still stand by a lot of what I said.

With this book, I want to take the time to hold a mirror up to a lot of ugly I see coming from the people whose fingers are on the big red button. Because despite the freedoms we still have, the system is broken. During the last midterm elections, 94 percent of Congress got reelected even though they have something like a 10 percent approval rating. Whether this disconnect is because a lot of people are too lazy or apathetic to vote; or because many people who would otherwise vote are too disillusioned with a system that puts the interests of rich corporations, their owners, and their lobbyists ahead of the people's best interest; or a combination of both, everyone—Democrat and Republican—seems to be in agreement that this country is halfway to hell.

And maybe because of all that, there seems to be an uptick of stupid. While, again, it's existed for centuries, stupid seems to be everywhere these days. Some believe it's because the human race is getting stupider and stupider with every passing year. Me? Apart from the paragraph above, I'd like to thank television, the Internet, social media, and the 24-hour news cycle for bringing more stupid to the public consciousness more efficiently than ever before. Thus, while I have a "historic chapter" on quotes that are from around 1990 and before, the giant bulk of these quotes will be from after 2000, and a big chunk of those from after 2010.

But first: How do I define *politician*? Everyone knows what the word means, but sometimes there can be a fine line between politician, government employee, and pundit. A politician, to me, is an individual who holds or has held an elected or high-up appointed position in local, state, or federal government, or is running for or has run for one. So while Jerry Falwell—the evangelist who started Liberty University, founded the Moral Majority and is a conservative idol—said a lot of dumb, political stuff (anyone else think the purple Teletubby was gay?), since he never ran for office, he's not a politician. However, Christine O'Donnell, who appeared as a pundit on *Politically Incorrect*, is a politician in my book, since she ran for Congress in Delaware. So what she says or said is fair game. What Falwell said would go in a book called *Sh\*t Pundits Say*, if anyone wanted to write one.

What about heads of special-interest groups? Unless they held office or ran for office, they go in the pundits drawer, too. So Tony Perkins, head of the Family Research Council (FRC) (a special special-interest organization that the Southern Poverty Law Center has labeled a hate group), I would consider a pundit if he were only ever head of the FRC. He served two terms as a Congressman in Louisiana and ran for state senator, so you'll find him among the politicians.

I must, at this time, offer an explanation to Republicans as to why most of the stupid has an R attached to the person dishing it out. When I looked for liberal stupid (and I found plenty), most of the quotes came from entertainers, not politicians. Also, a lot of the stupid had to do with Republican platforms, such as anti-LGBT statements and science denial. Which, sorry (not sorry), are stupid. And Bush and Palin, who get whole chapters, are walking stupid-machines.

Many of the "stupid quotes" in this book are said about sensitive subjects, such as abortion. As I've said, I'm not a supporter of abortions, but I don't think they should be illegal. I've included quotes that are biologically inaccurate (the senator that proposed we stick a camera down women's stomachs if they're considering abortion; FYI, Senator, the reproductive and the GI tracts don't connect), as well as completely insensitive remarks that lacked empathy for people in bad situations (for anyone who thinks women who are raped should "make the best of a bad situation," like Rick Santorum, I invite you to volunteer at a rape crisis call center for one day, or to imagine if someone you know was raped), and just the plain bizarre (fetuses masturbating in the womb? Really?). For issues such as the Affordable Care Act (ACA), I included quotes that were hyperbole or that showed conspiracies that didn't come true (Sarah Palin death panels, anyone?).

Anyway, I didn't organize this book chronologically. Instead, I attempted to categorize stupid, issue by issue. So we have stupid shit about global warming, health care, same-sex marriage, civil rights, and women. You'll also be entertained by stupid shit Democrats have said about taxing and spending, and stupid shit Republicans have said about the economy and women's rights.

But . . . some of the categories bleed into each other. Some stupid shit that was said about health care could also apply to civil rights, or women, or even the environment or the economy. So browse through and you're sure to find some favorites. And on another note, while this book is supposed to be humorous, a lot of the shit politicians say in here is not funny. At all. Several statements target women, minorities, and even bring up (meant to be an unfunny joke or not) policies that affect different groups of people, even denying them civil rights and liberties. I wish these were all in the historical chapter, but sadly, as I've said before, the world today is a pretty screwed-up place.

So without further ado, here are some of the stupidest, rudest, meanest quotes that have come out of the mouths of politicians in our time. Well, mostly in our time. First up, we have some truth denial: the first chapters of this book are dedicated to turning the pot shots on my faves, and the last chapter serves up "Sh*t I've Said." Hell, no one is above reproach.

# Chapter 1

## *Sh\*t Founding Fathers Said*

The Founders and early American leaders didn't say a lot of stupid shit. They *built* this country and shaped our political system. So this is a short chapter. No shit, they were smart, well-educated guys, unlike a lot of the morons we have running the game now. However, as I said in the introduction, these quotes were said in the days of yore when gaffes weren't well publicized and political leaders were so respected, that anything dumb they did say, or any misstatements, were probably hushed up. In fact, the bulk of these quotes came from their private records and were not aired out in public (we've come a long way from this to the shit-flinging contest that some recent debates have become, just saying). But one thing the Founders loved to do was insult each other. So here we go, some of the best Founding Fathers' insults:

**John Adams** was a pro at insults, and often cranky. A lethal combination. Here are his greatest:

### On Thomas Paine's Common Sense:

"What a poor, ignorant, malicious, short-sighted, crapulous mass."

### On George Washington:

"That Washington is not a scholar is certain. That he is too illiterate, unlearned, unread for his station is equally beyond dispute."

1

### On the City of Philadelphia:

"Phyladelphia [sic], with all its trade and wealth and regularity, is not Boston. The morals of our people are much better; their manners are more polite and agreeable . . . Our language is better, our taste is better, our persons are handsomer; our spirit is greater, our laws are wiser, our religion is superior, our education is better. We exceed them in every thing, but in a market."

### On Thomas Jefferson:

"His soul is poisoned with ambition."

———————

"An apostle of anarchy, a demagogue, a trickster."

### On Benjamin Franklin:

"His whole life has been one continued insult to good manners and to decency."

### On Alexander Hamilton:

"That bastard brat of a Scottish peddler! His ambition, his restlessness and all his grandiose schemes come, I'm convinced, from a superabundance of secretions, which he couldn't find enough whores to absorb!"

———————

"A superabundance of secretions which he could not find whores enough to draw off."

Some of America's other founders were almost as cranky as John Adams. . . .

### Thomas Jefferson, on Alexander Hamilton:

"I will not suffer my retirement to be clouded by the slanders of a man whose history, from the moment at which history can stoop to notice him, is a tissue of machinations against the liberty of the country, which has not only received and given him bread, but heaped its honor on his head."

### Alexander Hamilton, on Thomas Jefferson:

"He is not scrupulous about the means of success, nor very mindful of the truth, and . . . he is a contemptible hypocrite."

### Benjamin Franklin, on John Adams:

"He means well for his country, is always an honest man, often a wise one, but sometimes, and in some things, absolutely out of his senses."

### On inaugurations:

*Supreme Court Justice Joseph Story, on Andrew Jackson's inauguration guests:* "I never saw such a mixture. The reign of King Mob seemed triumphant."

---

*Congressman David Crockett (TN) on Martin Van Buren:* "It is said that at a year old he could laugh on one side of his face and cry on the other, at one and the same time."

# Chapter 2

## *Sh\*t JFK Said*

Here's a guy I love. Here's shit John F. Kennedy said; only a few quotes here I would say are stupid, most of them are more witty or clever, but it's all Kennedy (I've also included some quotes from his brothers that weren't included elsewhere. Basically, if what they said had to do with JFK or the Kennedy Dynasty, it goes here. If not, you can find it elsewhere):

### On being a Kennedy:

*Campaigning, during the 1958 Gridiron Dinner, JFK said:* "I just received the following wire from my generous Daddy: 'Dear Jack, Don't buy a single vote more than is necessary. I'll be damned if I'm going to pay for a landslide.'"

———

*John F. Kennedy, September 19, 1960, in an interview with Walter Cronkite:*

CRONKITE: Was it a conscious feeling on your part of taking Joe's place?

SENATOR KENNEDY: No, but I . . . I never would have run for office if he had lived.

———

*In a posthumous interview, airing on* 60 Minutes *on September 11, 2009, Ted Kennedy revealed the pressures of living up to his family name:* "I had a sit-down with my dad. He said, 'Now, Teddy, you have to make up your mind whether you want to have a constructive and positive attitude and influence on your time. And if you're not interested in a purposeful, useful, constructive life, I just want you to know I have other children that are out there that intend to have a purposeful and constructive life.'"

———

*In October 1960, responding to critics who questioned the amount of experience he had to be president, John F. Kennedy remarked:* "On this matter of experience, I had announced earlier this year that if successful I would not consider campaign contributions as a substitute for experience in appointing ambassadors. Ever since I made that statement I have not received one single cent from my father."

———

*In 1960, JFK told* Time *magazine journalist Hugh Sidey:* "I have no firsthand knowledge of the Depression. My family had one of the great fortunes of the world and it was worth more than ever then. We had bigger houses, more servants, we traveled more. About the only thing that I saw directly was when my father hired some extra gardeners just to give them a job so they could eat. I really did not learn about the Depression until I read about it at Harvard. My experience was the war. I can tell you about that."

### On winning:

*When JFK campaigned in Alaska and lost, but won Hawaii by a wide margin without visiting it, he said during his victory speech in 1960, Chicago (where he won the election by a small margin):* "Just think what my margin might have been if I had never left home at all."

---

*During the presidential campaign in 1960, JFK said:* "Do you realize the responsibility I carry? I'm the only person standing between Richard Nixon and the White House."

---

*Three years after winning by a margin of 0.2 percent, JFK told his audience at the AFL-CIO conference on November 16, 1963:* "Three years ago, and one week, by a landslide, the people of the United States elected me to the presidency of this country."

## On second place:

*In 1960, after being told he could get nominated as vice president easily, Kennedy retorted:* "Let's not talk so much about vice. I'm against vice in any form."

## On opponents:

*JFK often said:* "Forgive your enemies, but never forget their names." *(This may have been a favorite Kennedy family quote, as brother Bobby also has been quoted as saying it.)*

## On knowledge:

"You know nothing for sure . . . except the fact that you know nothing for sure." *(widely attributed to JFK, although no one's quite sure when he first said it)*

### On being a war hero:

*During a West Coast campaign trip in 1960, when a young boy asked JFK how he became a war hero, he replied:* "It was absolutely involuntary. They sank my boat."

———

*President John Kennedy, from a speech at the University of North Carolina, August 12, 1961:* "Those of you who regard my profession of political life with some disdain should remember that it made it possible for me to move from being an obscure lieutenant in the United States Navy to commander-in-chief in fourteen years with very little technical experience."

### On being married to Jackie:

*At a news conference at Palais de Chaillot in Paris, France, June 2, 1961, Kennedy started off his speech with:* "I do not think it entirely inappropriate to introduce myself to this audience. I am the man who accompanied Jacqueline Kennedy to Paris, and I have enjoyed it."

### On brothers:

*In response to mounting criticism of appointing his brother Robert attorney general, JFK said:* "I see nothing wrong with giving Robert some legal experience as Attorney General before he goes out to practice law." *(from Robert Kennedy's obituary in the* New York Times, *June 6, 1968)*

———

*At a rally in Fort Wayne, Indiana, May 18, 1968, alluding to his brother's success, Robert Kennedy told the crowd:* "It'll be less expensive just to send us to the White House. We'll arrange it so all 10

Sh*t Politicians Say

kids won't be there at once, and we won't need to expand the place. I'll send some of them away to school—and I'll make one of them Attorney General."

## On cities:

*President Kennedy, speaking at the Ohio Dinner in 1962, said:* "There is no city in the United States in which I get a warmer welcome and less votes than Columbus, Ohio."

## On standing your ground:

*During his remarks on founding a West German Peace Corps, June 24, 1963:* "Dante once said that the hottest places in hell are reserved for those who in a period of moral crisis maintain their neutrality." *(And people still believe Dante actually said this!)*

## President Kennedy, on bipartisanship:

*When motivating Democrats in Virginia to get out and vote at a speech at George Washington High School, August 24, 1960:* "I know that there are some Americans and some Democrats who say that they have now developed a wonderful arrangement in Washington. The Congress is Democratic and the President is Republican and nothing happens and isn't it wonderful. . . . I don't want legislation so cooled off that after it passes the House and the Senate that it is vetoed by a Republican President and sent back to die."

## On the Soviets:

*In response to the Soviet Union signing a peace treaty with East Germany to weaken US foreign policy, during a news conference in the State Department room, June 28, 1961:* "Khrushchev reminds me of the tiger hunter who has picked a place on the wall to hang the tiger's skin long before he has caught the tiger. This tiger has other ideas."

––––––––––

*Responding to Nixon's "Kitchen Debate" in Moscow, in 1960 John Kennedy quipped:* "Mr. Nixon may be very experienced in kitchen debates. So are a great many other married men I know."

## On time:

*Kennedy, addressing the National Association of Manufacturers on December 6, 1961:* "We must use time as a tool, not as a crutch."

## On J. Edgar Hoover:

*President John Kennedy on his reluctance to replace J. Edgar Hoover as FBI director, is rumored to have said:* "You don't fire God."

## On aliens:

*At a speech in 1959, JFK alluded to the nuclear arms race and the space race:* "I am sorry to say that there is too much point to the wisecrack that life is extinct on other planets because their scientists were more advanced than ours."

## On the presidency:

*To students interning in Washington DC, President Kennedy said:* "Sometimes I wish I just had a summer job here."

––––––––––

*Kennedy first passed this aphorism on to his press secretary, Pierre Salinger:* "Politics is like football; if you see daylight, go through the hole."

––––––––––

*When asked to comment on how the press was covering his administration, in July 1962, JFK replied:* "Well, I'm reading more and enjoying it less."

---

*At a speech in Indiana:* "I understand that this town suffered a misfortune this morning when a bank was robbed. I hope the *Indianapolis Star* doesn't say, 'Democrats arrive and bank robbed.' If they do, please don't believe them."

---

*A quote widely attributed to President Kennedy:* "Mothers all want their sons to grow up to be president, but they don't want them to become politicians in the process."

---

*Kennedy in 1961:* "The day before my inauguration President Eisenhower told me, 'You'll find that no easy problems ever come to the President of the United States. If they are easy to solve, somebody else has solved them.' I found that hard to believe, but now I know it is true."

---

*On being president, Kennedy often said:* "The pay is good and I can walk to work."

## On problem solving:

*After handling the Bay of Pigs crisis in 1963, JFK said:* "Look at that, I have a total fiasco and my poll ratings go up. What am I going to do to get them up further?"

### On women in politics:

*Speaking to a United Nations delegation of women, December 11, 1961, JFK said:* "I'm always rather nervous about how you talk about women who are active in politics, whether they want to be talked about as women or as politicians."

### On education:

*Receiving an honorary degree from Yale University, speaking at their commencement, on June 11, 1962, JFK remarked:* "It might be said now that I have the best of both worlds. A Harvard education and a Yale degree."

### What JFK might say about quotes in the rest of this book:

*President John Kennedy, at that same Yale University commencement in 1962:* "The great enemy of the truth is very often not the lie—deliberate, contrived, and dishonest—but the myth—persistent, persuasive, and unrealistic."

### On Republicans:

*A reporter asked JFK on July 17, 1963:* "The Republican National Committee recently adopted a resolution saying you were pretty much of a failure. How do you feel about that?" *He replied:* "I assume it passed unanimously."

---

*After Democrats won gubernatorial races in New York and New Jersey during his first year of office, JFK commented in November 1961:* "They won because they were effective candidates. But they ran as Democrats. And I believe that it indicates that the American people believe that the candidates and parties in those areas, as well as nationally, are committed to progress. So I am happy, and I suppose some day we will lose and then I'll have to eat those words."

Sh*t Politicians Say

## On music:

*When asked what his favorite song was, JFK often answered:* "I think *Hail to the Chief* has a nice ring to it."

## If only:

*President John Kennedy in February 1961:* "It has recently been suggested that whether I serve one or two terms in the presidency, I will find myself at the end of that period at what might be called the awkward age, too old to begin a new career and too young to write my memoirs."

## On assassinations:

*In his book* With Kennedy, *JFK's press secretary Pierre Salinger quoted the president as saying:* "If anyone is crazy enough to want to kill a president of the United States, he can do it. All he must be prepared to do is give his life for the president's."

# Chapter 3

## Sh*t Democrats Say

Here, you'll find the Biden-isms, the Obama-isms, and the stupid, smug stuff said that is from the jackass side of the aisle.

### Creating more gridlock:

*Representative Harry Reid (D-NV), arguing to raise the number of votes needed from 51 percent (strict majority rule) to 60 percent, December 8, 2006:* "As majority leader, I intend to run the Senate with respect for the rules and for the minority rights the rules protect. The Senate was not established to be efficient. Sometimes the rules get in the way of efficiency."

### Hi there:

*Barack Obama, campaigning in Sunrise, Florida, 2008:* "How's it going, Sunshine?"

### True story:

*Alben Barkley, VP of the United States, 1949 to 1953, once said:* "The best audience is intelligent, well educated, and a little drunk."

### On drugs:

*Bill Clinton, at a candidates' forum on WCBS, while running for president, March 29, 1992:* "When I was in England, I experimented

15

with marijuana a time or two, and I didn't like it. I didn't inhale it, and never tried it again."

### Guessing people's sexuality:

*Brian Schweitzer (governor of Montana), on Eric Cantor, June 18, 2014:* "If you were just a regular person, you turned on the TV, and you saw Eric Cantor talking, I would say—and I'm fine with gay people, that's all right. But my gaydar is 60 to 70 percent." *(He later apologized.)*

### On tourism:

*Harry Reid, December 2, 2008, as part of the official dedication to the Capitol Visitor Center:* "My staff tells me not to say this, but I'm going to say it anyway, in the summer because of the heat and high humidity, you could literally smell the tourists coming into the Capitol. It may be descriptive but it's true."

### On (not) campaigning:

*Bill Clinton, via the Asheville* Citizen-Times *(Asheville, North Carolina), October 12, 2014:* "The great thing about not being president anymore is you can say whatever you want. Unless your wife might run for something."

### Seeing the dead:

*After the 1989 San Francisco earthquake, Senator Barbara Boxer (D-CA), said in response:* "Those who survived the San Francisco earthquake said, 'Thank God, I'm still alive.' But, of course, those who died, their lives will never be the same again."

### And even Obama sees dead people:

*In a Memorial Day address in 2008 in Las Cruces, New Mexico, Barack Obama said:* "Fallen heroes—and I see many of them in the audience here today."

### Nice comeback:

*Barack Obama, at the 2008 Al Smith Dinner:* "Who is Barack Obama? Contrary to the rumors you have heard, I was not born in a manger. I was actually born on Krypton and sent here by my father Jor-El to save the Planet Earth."

### The wrath of the nerds:

*President Obama, mixing up* Star Wars *and* Star Trek *references while discussing working with Republicans in Congress, March 1, 2013:* "Even though most people agree . . . I'm presenting a fair deal, the fact that they don't take it means that I should somehow do a Jedi mind-meld with these folks and convince them to do what's right."

### On socialism:

*Rep. Maxine Waters, at a Congressional hearing about oil, May 23, 2008:* "Guess what this liberal would be all about? This liberal will be about socializing . . . uh, um . . . Would be about, basically, taking over, and the government running all of your companies."

### When you need new material, be careful whom you ask:

*President Barack Obama, at the 2009 Radio and Television Correspondents' Dinner:* "I have to admit, though, it wasn't easy coming up with fresh material for this dinner. A few nights ago, I was up tossing and turning, trying to figure out exactly what to say. Finally, when I couldn't get back to sleep, I rolled over and asked Brian Williams what he thought."

### Giving Republicans ammo:

*In an interview with George Stephanopoulos on ABC about the 2008 presidential race amid allegations that Obama was Muslim, he remarked:* "What I was suggesting—you're absolutely right that John McCain has not talked about my Muslim faith. . . ."

*(Stephanopoulos corrected Obama by saying "your Christian faith," which Obama quickly clarified.)*

----

*Sen. John Kerry, March 19, 2004, on voting against a military funding bill for US troops in Iraq:* "I actually did vote for the $87 billion, before I voted against it."

### Trying not to swear:

*Joe Biden, to the Harvard student body vice president, October 3, 2014:* "Isn't it a bitch? I mean . . . excuse me. The vice president thing."

### Obama on baseball:

*(The prez said this one-liner June 25, 2015, in Boston after the Red Sox traded their beloved slugger Kevin Youkilis to the Chicago White Sox, Obama's hometown team):* "And finally, Bos, I just want to say thank you for Youkilis." *(The line drew boos from the audience, needless to say!)*

### Obama's comebacks for opponents:

*At a rally in Las Vegas, September 18, 2008:* "Yesterday, John McCain actually said that if he's president that he'll take on, and I quote, 'the old boys network in Washington.' Now I'm not making this up. This is somebody who's been in Congress for twenty-six years, who put seven of the most powerful Washington lobbyists in charge of his campaign. And now he tells us that he's the one who's going to take on the old boys' network. The old boys' network? In the McCain campaign that's called a staff meeting. Come on!"

----

*Poking fun at Sarah Palin at the Al Smith Dinner, 2012:* "I do love the Waldorf Astoria, though. You know, I hear that from the doorstep you can see all the way to the Russian Tea Room."

### Low blow:

*Rep. Pete Stark (D-WI), to a constituent, September 13, 2009:* "I wouldn't dignify you by peeing on your leg. It wouldn't be worth wasting the urine."

### On making friends in Congress:

*Barack Obama, at the 2013 White House Correspondents' Dinner:* "Some folks still don't think I spend enough time with Congress. 'Why don't you get a drink with Mitch McConnell?' they ask. Really? Why don't *you* get a drink with Mitch McConnell?"

---

*Barack Obama, on attacks against him at the Republican convention, September 2008:* "I've been called worse on the basketball court."

### Roasting the press:

*Barack Obama, at the 2012 White House Correspondents' Dinner:* "The White House Correspondents' Dinner is known as the prom of Washington DC—a term coined by political reporters who clearly never had the chance to go to an actual prom."

### Barack Obama, roastmaster:

*Roasting his future chief of staff Rahm Emanuel in 2005:* "But the truth is when you really get to know Rahm, he does have a softer side, Amy will attest to this; very few people know, I think, know prior to this evening that he studied ballet for a few years. In fact, he was the first to adopt Machiavelli's *The Prince* for dance. It was an intriguing piece, as you can imagine, there were a lot of kicks below the waist."

---

*At the 2012 Al Smith Dinner:* "Everyone please take your seats, or else Clint Eastwood will yell at them."

---

*On John McCain's attacks, Raleigh, North Carolina, October 29, 2008:* "Now, because he knows that his economic theories don't work, he's been spending these last few days calling me every name in the book. Lately he's called me a socialist for wanting to roll back the Bush tax cuts for the wealthiest Americans so we can finally give tax relief to the middle class. I don't know what's next. By the end of the week he'll be accusing me of being a secret communist because I shared my toys in kindergarten. I shared my peanut butter and jelly sandwich."

### Getting caught at a strip club:

*Marion Barry, Mayor of Washington, DC, in response to getting arrested January 19, 1990 at a strip club for possession of crack:* "First, it was not a strip bar, it was an erotic club. And second, what can I say? I'm a night owl."

### Not a scandal, but sounds way wrong:

"Folks, I can tell you I've known eight presidents, three of them intimately." *(Joe Biden, August 22, 2012)*

### TMI:

*Joe Biden, referring to his wife, Jill, while speaking at a National Teacher of the Year reception, April 27, 2010:* "I've been sleeping with a teacher for a long time. But it's always been the same teacher."

---

Sh*t Politicians Say

*Ted Kennedy, while dressed as Barney the Dinosaur at a 1993 Christmas party (noted in the book* The Kennedy Men*):* "They don't call me Tyrannosaurus Sex for nothing."

———

*Ex-Congressman Eric Massa (D-NY), talking to Glenn Beck on his show on March 9, 2010, after resigning amid allegations that he sexually harassed his aides:* "Now, they're saying I groped a male staffer. Yes, I did. Not only did I grope him, I tickled him until he couldn't breathe and four guys jumped on top of me. It was my 50th birthday."

## More misspeaking:

*This quote from Ted Kennedy, given at a broadcast speech about education, has been often cited as a textbook Freudian slip:* "Our national interest ought to be to encourage the breast, best, and the brightest to complete their education, to be involved in the life and the community of . . . uh . . . this . . . uh . . . of this country."

## Here's Bill!:

*Bill Clinton, speaking on January 26, 1998, after getting caught having an affair with Monica Lewinsky:* "I want to say one thing to the American people. I want you to listen to me. I'm going to say this again: I did not have sexual relations with that woman, Miss Lewinsky. I never told anybody to lie, not a single time; never. These allegations are false. And I need to go back to work for the American people."

———

*Bill Clinton's Grand Jury testimony, August 17, 1998:* "It depends upon what the meaning of the word 'is' is."

———

*Clinton, explaining his physical contact with Lewinsky, January 17, 1998:* "I embraced her, I put my arms around her, I may have even kissed her on the forehead. There was nothing sexual about it. I was trying to help her calm down and trying to reassure her."

———

*Defending his denial of the Lewinsky affair, August 17, 1998:* "Now, if someone had asked me on that day, are you having any kind of sexual relations with Ms. Lewinsky, that is, asked me a question in the present tense, I would have said no. And it would have been completely true."

## Not Bill:

*Joe Biden, April 17, 2014, repurposing an old joke:* "Jill is probably right. I think I'd have the same attitude did I not sleep with a community college professor every night. Oh, the same one, the same one. The same one."

## Joe Biden, on SCOTUS:

*On when a Republican president got to nominate a Supreme Court Justice, June 25, 1992:* "It is my view that if a Supreme Court justice resigns tomorrow or within the next several weeks, or resigns at the end of the summer, President [George H. W.] Bush should consider following the practice of a majority of his predecessors and not, and not, and not, name a nominee until after the November election is completed."

———

*But when the shoe is on the other foot—in an op-ed piece in the* New York Times, *March 3, 2016, called "The Senate's Duty on a Supreme Court nominee," Biden wrote of Congress's resistance to Obama's choosing a new justice:* "It is an unprecedented act of obstruction. And it risks a stain on the legacy of all those complicit in carrying out this plan. I would ask my friends and colleagues—and all those who love the Senate—to think long and hard before going down this road."

### Joe Biden, giving condolences:

*Speaking about the Irish Prime Minister Brian Cowen in Washington DC at a 2010 St. Patrick's Day speech, Biden mentioned that he recently lost a parent:* "His mom lived in Long Island for ten years or so. God rest her soul. And although she's . . . wait . . . your mom's still . . . your mom's still alive. Your dad passed. God bless her soul."

### Insulting diplomats:

*Joe Biden, speaking to a group of Turkish-American and Azerbaijani-American donors, April 27, 2012:* "I guess what I'm trying to say without boring you too long at breakfast—and you all look dull as hell, I might add. The dullest audience I have ever spoken to. Just sitting there, staring at me. Pretend you like me!"

### Joe Biden, on Obama's big stick (referencing Theodore Roosevelt's famous quote, "Speak softly and carry a big stick; you will go far"):

"I promise you, the president has a big stick. I promise you." *(April 26, 2012)*

### Obama, on Obamacare (and shooting yourself in the foot):

*Barack Obama, about his plan to reform health care, July 20, 2009:* "The reforms we seek would bring greater competition, choice, savings, and inefficiencies to our health care system."

*Jerry Brown, former governor of California, on welfare:*

"The conventional viewpoint says we need a jobs program and we need to cut welfare. Just the opposite! We need more welfare and fewer jobs." *(February 3, 2011)*

*Obama on the campaign trail in 2008, after being asked a foreign policy question by a reporter while visiting a diner in Pennsylvania:*

"Why can't I just eat my waffle?"

*I Think I'll pass on your "spinach dip":*

*In her grand jury testimony, September 22, 1998, Monica Lewinsky was asked whether the stain on her infamous blue dress was semen. She replied:* "It could have been spinach dip or something."

*On (not) being under sniper fire:*

*Hillary Clinton, recalling her visit to Bosnia as first lady in 1996:* "I remember landing under sniper fire. There was supposed to be some kind of a greeting ceremony at the airport, but instead we just ran with our heads down to get into the vehicles to get to our base." *(Other accounts said there was no threat of gunfire. Clinton later said she "misspoke.")*

*Jesse Jackson, on wanting to "cut off" candidate Obama:*

"See, Barack been um, talking down to black people on this faith based . . . I wanna cut his nuts off." *(Reverend Jackson thought his microphone was off when speaking before a segment on Fox News, July 6, 2008.)*

*On rage:*

*Bill Clinton, at a Washington DC construction site, yelling at an aide on February 16, 1993, not knowing his microphone was on:* "Come on.

Come on. Listen, goddamn it. Come here. You can't do that. You can't take me out here with a mayor and a congresswoman and push them back."

---

*Pete Stark, after interviewer Jan Helfeld asked him in 2008 to explain his statement on national debt:* "We're done. Get out of here! No! I'm done! Get out! Listen, you get the f*ck out of here or I'll throw you out the window."

---

*Sen. Mary Landrieu (D-LA), speaking on* This Week with George Stephanopoulos, *September 4, 2005, about criticism on the handling of Hurricane Katrina:* "If one person criticizes [the local authorities' relief efforts] or says one more thing, including the president of the United States, he will hear from me. One more word about it after this show airs, and I . . . I might likely have to punch him, literally."

## Barack Obama, on small-town America:

*Speaking on April 11, 2008, at a San Francisco fund-raiser about his troubles winning over some small-town, working-class voters:* "It's not surprising, then, they get bitter, they cling to guns or religion or antipathy to people who aren't like them or anti-immigrant sentiment or antitrade sentiment as a way to explain their frustrations."

## Insulting veterans:

*Rep. Pete Stark (D-CA), responding to a veteran's call on May 6, 2004, about HR 627, a bill condemning abuses of Iraqi prisoners and calling for those responsible to be brought to justice; Stark voted against the resolution:* "Dan, this is Congressman 'Pete' Stark, and I just got your fax and you don't know what you're talking about.

So if you care about enlisted people you wouldn't have voted for that thing, either. But probably somebody put you up to this, and I'm not sure who it was, but I doubt if you could spell half the words in the letter. Somebody wrote it for you so I don't pay much attention to it, but I'll call you back later and let you tell me more about why you think you're such a great G**damn hero and why you think that this general and the defense department who forced these poor enlisted (bitter laughter) guys to do what they should shouldn't be held to account. That's the issue. So if you want to stick it to a bunch of enlisted guys have your way, but if you want to get to the bottom of people who forced this awful program in . . . Iraq, then you should understand more about it than you obviously do. Thanks."

————

*Sen. John Kerry (D-MA), botching a joke about President Bush getting us stuck in Iraq, October 30, 2006, in response to White House press secretary Tony Snow:* "You know, education—if you make the most of it—you study hard, you do your homework, and you make an effort to be smart, you can do well. If you don't, you get stuck in Iraq."

### On how old our country is:

*Sheila Jackson Lee, March 12, 2014:* "Maybe I should offer a good thanks to the distinguished members of the majority, the Republicans, my chairman and others, for giving us an opportunity to have a deliberative constitutional discussion that reinforces the sanctity of this nation and how well it is that we have lasted some 400 years, operating under a Constitution that clearly defines what is constitutional and what is not." *(When corrected, she accused her critic of trying to make her look foolish.)*

### Can trains really travel over water?:

*Barack Obama, September 22, 2011, who thought we had a railroad running from North America to Europe, apparently:* "We used to have the best infrastructure in the world here in America. We're the country that built the Intercontinental Railroad."

### I don't think that means what you think it means:

*Barack Obama, on* The Tonight Show *with Jay Leno, talking about his love of bowling, March 20, 2009:* "No, no. I have been practicing. . . . I bowled a 129. It's like—it was like Special Olympics, or something." *(He called the Special Olympics later that night to apologize.)*

### Obama's position:

*Vice President Joe Biden on jobs, October 15, 2008, via MSNBC:* "The number-one job facing the middle class, and it happens to be, as Barack says, a three-letter word: jobs. J-O-B-S."

———

*Joe Biden, referring to Barack Obama at the beginning of the 2008 Democratic primary campaign, January 31, 2007:* "I mean, you got the first mainstream African-American who is articulate and bright and clean and a nice-looking guy. I mean, that's a story-book, man."

———

*Senate Democratic Leader Harry Reid, in the book* Game Change, *2008,* argued that Obama's race would actually help his campaign: "A light skinned African-American with no Negro dialect, unless he wanted to have one." *(He apologized after the book's release.)*

### Did we forget something?:

"Stand up, Chuck, let 'em see ya." *(Joe Biden, attempting to coax paralyzed Senator Chuck Graham out of his wheelchair, Columbia, Missouri, September 12, 2008)*

### Barack Obama, honoring veteran Jared Monti, who was killed in 2006:

"I had the great honor of seeing some of you because a comrade of yours, Jared Monti, was the first person who I was able to award the Medal of Honor to who actually came back and wasn't receiving it posthumously." *(Obama apparently didn't have his dates straight, as he awarded Monti a posthumous Medal of Honor on June 23, 2009.)*

### Nancy Pelosi, urging Congress to pass the affordable care act, and not helping her case:

"But we have to pass the bill so that you can find out what is in it, away from the fog of the controversy." *(March 9, 2010, Washington DC)*

### On respect:

*Barack Obama, paying tribute to the iconic singer Aretha Franklin, then flubbing one of her lyrics:* "R-S-P-E-C-T." *(New York City, March 6, 2014)*

### Accents:

*Joe Biden, in a private remark to an Indian-American man caught on C-SPAN, June 6, 2006:* "You cannot go to a 7-11 or a Dunkin' Donuts unless you have a slight Indian accent. . . . I'm not joking."

---

Sh*t Politicians Say

*Joe Biden, imitating an Indian accent, again, January 26, 2012:* "Even call centers . . .which rushed overseas in the hundreds of thousands," *Mr Biden began, then melting into what appeared to be an Indian accent.* "How many times do you get the call, 'I like to talk to you about your credit card?'"

### On ATMs:

*On May 20, 2010, Sen. Ben Nelson (D-NE) confided to CBS News that he had never used an ATM:* "It's true, I don't know how to use one. But I could learn how to do it just like I've . . . I swipe to get my own gas, buy groceries. I know about the holograms." (*However, the* Omaha World-Herald *notes that after mentioning the holograms,* "Nelson clarified that he meant the barcodes on products read by automatic scanners in the check-out lanes at stores such as Lowe's and Menard's.")

### On seniors:

*Harry Reid, April 18, 2012, arguing to pass a bill reforming the US Postal Service, by saying:* "Seniors love getting junk mail. It's sometimes their only way of communicating or feeling like they're part of the real world."

### On death tolls:

*Barack Obama, on a Kansas tornado that killed twelve people, May 9, 2007:* "In case you missed it, this week, there was a tragedy in Kansas. Ten thousand people died—an entire town destroyed."

### On the fifty (?) US states:

*Barack Obama, at a campaign event in Beaverton, Oregon, May 9, 2008:* "I've now been in fifty-seven states—I think one left to go."

### On animal taxonomy:

*Al Gore, in 1992, attacking President George H. W. Bush by saying:* "A zebra does not change its spots."

### On three-way ties for last place:

*Sen. Joseph Lieberman (D-CT) to CNN's Wolf Blitzer, on his momentum leading up to the New Hampshire Primary, 2004:* "Be excited. This is Joementum here in New Hampshire." *(He characterized his fifth-place finish as a "three-way split decision for third place."* Urban Dictionary *honored him by making* joementum *a word, meaning "something that isn't going anywhere.")*

### A president needs to know his place:

*President Obama, on being in Hawaii, his home state, November 16, 2011:* "When I meet with world leaders, what's striking—whether it's in Europe or here in Asia. . . ."

### President Barack America!:

*Joe Biden, at his first campaign rally with Barack Obama in Springfield, Illinois, August 23, 2008, after being announced as his running mate, introduced him this way:* "A man I'm proud to call my friend. A man who will be the next president of the United States—Barack America!"

### On mummies:

*Bill Clinton, on "Juanita," a newly discovered Incan mummy on display at the National Geographic museum:* "If I were a single man, I might ask that mummy out. That's a good-looking mummy."

### 1930s television:

*Vice President Joe Biden in an interview with Katie Couric about the Recession, September 22, 2008:* "When the stock market crashed,

Franklin D. Roosevelt got on the television and didn't just talk about the, you know, the princes of greed. He said, 'Look, here's what happened.'"

### About those hijackers:

*Rep. Alan Grayson (D-FL), on the prospects of Republicans taking back control of Congress, May 21, 2010:* "Why would you want to put people in charge of government who just don't want to do it? I mean, you wouldn't expect to see al Qaeda members as pilots."

### Al Gore, on who created the Internet:

*In an interview with CNN's Wolf Blitzer, March 9, 1999:* "During my service in the United States Congress, I took the initiative in creating the Internet. I took the initiative in moving forward a whole range of initiatives that have proven to be important to our country's economic growth and environmental protection, improvements in our educational system."

### On cities in Missouri:

*While in Kansas City, Missouri, to the DNC via satellite, August 25, 2008, Barack Obama said:* "I'm here with the Girardo family here in St. Louis."

### On honesty:

*Sen. Chris Dodd (D-CT), as he approached the end of a reelection campaign, on the* Don Imus Show: "Eight more days and I can start telling the truth again."

---

*Hillary Clinton, at a Democratic fund-raiser in Iowa, August 14, 2015, joking after she handed over her emails to the FBI:* "You may have seen I recently launched a Snapchat account. I love it. I love it. Those messages disappear all by themselves."

## We hope so:

*Edwin W. Edwards, on running against Grand Dragon of the KKK David Duke for governor of Louisiana in 1991:* "I could not lose unless I was caught in bed with a dead girl or a live boy."

## Guess not:

"My choice early in life was either to be a piano player in a whore house or a politician. And to tell the truth, there's hardly any difference." *(Harry S. Truman, verified by snopes)*

## On getting caught:

*November 4, 2008—Illinois Gov. Rod Blagojevich was recorded in a federal wiretap trying to sell Barack Obama's Senate seat. The day before his arrest, he invited authorities to tape his conversations, saying there is "nothing but sunshine hanging over me":* "I'm just not giving it up for f***in' nothing. I'm not gonna do it. And, and I can always use it. I can parachute me there." . . . "Give this motherf****r Obama his senator? F**k him. For nothing. F**k him."

Sh*t Politicians Say

WHAT A WASTE IT IS TO LOSE ONE'S MIND

# Chapter 4

## *Sh\*t Republicans Say*

Hoo boy! This is a long one! Republicans have said more than their fair share of crap. Some of it is stupid, or ignorant; some of it is a flat-out lie, a flip-flop, or just mean-spirited fun (I did get a kick out of some of these, though, like Mike Huckabee imagining Hillary Clinton getting rocketed to the moon). As I said in my Intro, the crazier, loonier quotes come from the elephants' side of the aisle, as far as politicians go. If you want to see me bash Democrats and liberals more than I just did, I'll have to put out a *Sh\*t Entertainers Say* book.

### Testing, testing, Ronald Reagan's infamous 1984 sound check for an NPR interview:

"I've signed legislation that will outlaw Russia forever. Bombing starts in five minutes." *(The press, and the Russian Embassy, got ahold of it, causing an embarrassment to the administration.)*

### About the other side of the aisle:

*Mike Huckabee, at the presidential GOP debate, November 28, 2007:* "Whether we need to send somebody to Mars, I don't know. But I'll tell you what, if we do, I've got a few suggestions, and maybe Hillary could be on the first rocket."

———

*Ted Cruz, GOP dinner in Howell, Michigan, June 3, 2015:* "Vice President Joe Biden. You know, the nice thing is that you don't even need a punch line."

———

*Bobby Jindal, from "GOP Needs Action, Not Navel-Gazing," in* Politico, *June 18, 2013:* "Because the left wants: The government to explode; to pay everyone; to hire everyone; they believe that money grows on trees; the earth is flat; the industrial age, factory-style government is a cool new thing; debts don't have to be repaid; people of faith are ignorant and uneducated; unborn babies don't matter; pornography is fine; traditional marriage is discriminatory; 32 oz. sodas are evil; red meat should be rationed; rich people are evil unless they are from Hollywood or are liberal Democrats; the Israelis are unreasonable; trans-fat must be stopped; kids trapped in failing schools should be patient; wild weather is a new thing; moral standards are passé; government run health care is high quality; the IRS should violate our constitutional rights; reporters should be spied on; Benghazi was handled well; the Second Amendment is outdated; and the First one has some problems too."

---

*Adam Putnam, taking back an untrue statement he repeated about Obama offering free cell phones to poor people, (via* Politifact, *October 31, 2012):* "About those cell phones: I'd heard about the YouTube video, wasn't aware it was disclaimed. Won't happen again." *(He made the original statement at a Romney campaign rally, and backpedaled when the information was proven to be false. A low-income phone program is available through the FCC, but it's not "free.")*

### On political opposition:

*Senator candidate Sharron Angle (R-NV), at an event in Utah, September 18, 2010:* "If this Congress keeps going the way it is, people are really looking toward those Second Amendment remedies and saying, 'My goodness, what can we do to turn this country around?' And I'll tell ya, the first thing they need to do is take Harry Reid out."

———

*Mitch McConnell, on CNN's* State of the Union, *October 23, 2011:* "Their [Democrats] story line is that there must be some villain out there who's keeping this administration from succeeding." *(This after saying in* The National Journal *on November 4, 2010:* "The single most important thing we want to achieve is for President Obama to be a one-term president."*)*

### Ted Cruz, filibustering, September 23, 2013:

"I remember in the debate over drones, Senator Rubio began quoting from rap lyrics, and I'll confess to being clueless enough that I didn't even know what he was referencing. I was sure it was something far too hip for me to know."

### Chris Christie to Donald Trump, GOP debate, October 28, 2015:

"Even in New Jersey, what you're doing is called rude."

### Yo Mama:

*Donald Trump, about Marco Rubio, Fox News GOP debate, March 3, 2016:* "This little guy has lied so much about my record . . . you haven't employed even one person."

———

"Trump Steaks." *(Rubio's reply to the above, March 3, 2016)*

———

*Trump:* "Little Marco." *(Fox News GOP debate, March 3, 2016)*

———

*Rubio:* "Big Don" *(March 3, 2016)*

***Donald Trump, referring to his alleged penis size during the Fox News GOP debate, March 3, 2016:***

"I also happen to call him a lightweight, OK, and I really said that, and I'd like to take that back, he's not that much of a lightweight, and as far as, I have to say this . . . he hit my hands. Nobody has ever hit my hands, I have never heard this: 'Look at those hands, aren't they small hands?' And, he referred to my hands, if they're small, something else must be small. I guarantee you there's no problem, there isn't."

***Ted Cruz, July 9, 2013, commenting on Romney's campaign (pretty much):***

"Now, if you look at the last election, I think in 2012 the reason Republicans lost can be summed up in two words: 47 percent."

***Mitt Romney, on Reagan-Bush:***

*Addressing Ted Kennedy during a debate in the 1994 Massachusetts Senate Campaign:* "I mentioned nothing about politics or your position at all. I talked about what I'd do to help strengthen families, and you talked about Reagan-Bush. Look, I was an independent during the time of Reagan-Bush. I'm not trying to return to Reagan-Bush."

———

*Speaking at the annual Reagan Lecture at the Ronald Reagan Library in May 2010:* "I'm optimistic about the future because I recognize that there is a growing awakening among the American people that this administration has put us on the wrong track and that the principles that Ronald Reagan espoused are as true today as they were when he spoke them."

**Bob Dole, on parenting (during his run against Clinton, in New York magazine, April 29, 1996):**

"If something happened along the route and you had to leave your children with Bob Dole or Bill Clinton, I think you would probably leave them with Bob Dole."

**On their base:**

*Donald Trump, after winning the Nevada caucus, February 26, 2016:* "I love the poorly educated! They are the smartest people, the most loyal people."

———

*While running for president, then GOP presidential nominee John McCain nearly slipped up addressing his supporters in Moon Township, Pennsylvania, on October 21, 2008:* "You know, I think you may have noticed that Senator Obama's supporters have been saying some pretty nasty things about Western Pennsylvania lately. And you know, I couldn't agree with them more. I couldn't disagree with you. I couldn't agree with you more than the fact that Western Pennsylvania is the most patriotic, most god-loving, most, most patriotic part of America, and this is a great part of the country."

———

*Donald Trump, at a 2016 rally broadcast on* C-SPAN Road to the White House: "I'm self-funding my campaign, other than the little tiny ones where they send in, you know, women send in, you know we had a woman send in seven dollars and fifty-nine cents. What do you do? How can you send the money back? You know it's a nice, it's a cute, it's beautiful, they feel invested in your campaign." *(re-aired on* Late Night with John Oliver, *Sunday, February 28, 2016)*

## On hunting:

*Campaigning in Indianapolis in 2007, Mitt Romney described himself as a lifelong game hunter:* "I purchased a gun when I was a young man. I've been a hunter pretty much all my life." *(He had only hunted twice according to his campaign aides: once when he was a teenager and another time at a 2006 Republican fund-raiser. When caught in his fib, he backpedaled and said:* "I've never been a big game hunter. I've made that very clear. I've always been a rodent and rabbit hunter. Small varmints, if you will.")

## Sen. Lindsey Graham, breaking the Golden Rule (never EVER say you're raising taxes!!!):

*During his breach with the NORQUIST antitax pledge, June 21, 2012:* "We need to raise taxes to get our nation out of debt."

## On insulting your donors:

*Rick Perry, suggesting on his first day campaigning for president, in Cedar Rapids, Iowa, on August 15, 2011, that Federal Reserve Chairman Ben Bernanke may be a traitor to his country:* "If this guy prints more money between now and the election. I don't know what y'all would do to him in Iowa, but we . . . we would treat him pretty ugly down in Texas. Printing more money to play politics at this particular time in American history is almost treacherous—or treasonous in my opinion."

## Rick Santorum, on gerrymandering:

"Certainly from the standpoint of a Republican, it's a winner. Republicans will come out ahead in Pennsylvania in every election. The way Democrats win, they have two big cities with huge concentrations of voters—and then overwhelm the rest of the state. All of a sudden, a Republican can win—and would probably routinely win—all but three or four congressional districts in Pennsylvania. It would turn it from a state Democrats rely on, as part of the base, to a state that they're gonna lose under almost any scenario." *(Washington DC, September 20, 2011)*

### Mitt Romney, on dogs:

"PETA is not happy that my dog likes fresh air." *(responding to criticism in 2007 from People for the Ethical Treatment of Animals, following revelations that he had once strapped the family dog to the roof of his car during a twelve-hour road trip)*

### Paul Ryan, on Ayn Rand:

*In a 2005 speech to the Atlas Society, a group of Ayn Rand fans, he said:* "I grew up reading Ayn Rand and it taught me quite a bit about who I am and what my value systems are and what my beliefs are. It's inspired me so much that it's required reading in my office for all my interns and my staff."

———

*Later, in an April 2012 interview with the* National Review, *he flip-flopped:* "I reject her [Ayn Rand's] philosophy. It's an atheist philosophy. It reduces human interactions down to mere contracts and it is antithetical to my worldview. If somebody is going to try to paste a person's view on epistemology to me, then give me Thomas Aquinas. Don't give me Ayn Rand."

### Ted Cruz, on honesty:

*In an interview with radio host Mark Levin, February 13, 2013:* "In the thirteen months I've been in the Senate, it has become apparent to me the single thing that Republican politicians hate and fear the most, and that is when they're forced to tell the truth. It makes their heads explode."

*Lindsey Graham, on honesty et al:*

"Dishonest, which is Hillary Clinton in the eyes of the American people, beats crazy. Dishonest loses to normal. So, let's just pick somebody out of the phone book if we have to." *(January 21, 2016)*

*Mitt Romney at the Buddy Brew Coffee shop, talking with unemployed Floridians:*

"I should tell my story. I'm also unemployed." *(June 16, 2011)*

*Rick Wiles, on Supreme Court Justice Antonin Scalia's death (note: he's speculating that Obama had Justice Scalia killed as a pagan, Lupercalia sacrifice):*

"[The assassins] deliberately left the pillow on his face as a message to everybody else: 'Don't mess with us, we can murder a justice and get away with it.' And I assure you, there's a lot of frightened officials in Washington today, deep down they know, the regime murdered a justice. . . . This is the way a dictatorial, fascist, police state regime takes control of a nation." *(February 15, 2016)*

*Rep. Steve King believes Obama's fifty-seven-states gaffe has a secret meaning! (see previous chapter):*

"And I know the president made the mistake one day of saying he had visited all fifty-seven states, and I'm well aware that there are not fifty-seven states in this country, although there are fifty-seven members of OIC, the Islamic states in the world. Perhaps there was some confusion whether he'd been to all fifty-seven Islamic states as opposed to all fifty US states. But nonetheless, we have an obligation to the fifty American states, not the fifty-seven Muslim, Islamic states. Our oath we took is in this body, in this House. And it's to the people of America. And it's not to the Muslim Brotherhood, who may very well take over Egypt and once they

Sh*t Politicians Say

do, they are bent upon setting up a caliphate around the world, including the United States. And this administration will been . . . complicit in helping people who wants . . . to destroy our country." *(June 17, 2011, speaking on the House floor, Washington DC)*

### Ted Cruz, on Obama, the kidnapper (note: he was trying to make a joke):

"So this afternoon President Obama has invited the Senate Republicans to the White House. So after leaving here, I'm going to be going to the White House. I will make a request. If I'm never seen again, please send a search and rescue team. I very much hope by tomorrow morning I don't wake up amidst the Syrian rebels." *(October 11, 2013)*

### About their side of the aisle:

*Rick Perry, fumbling over his attack lines against Romney at a GOP presidential debate, September 22, 2011:* "Is it the Mitt Romney that was on the side of—against the Second Amendment before he was for the Second Amendment? . . . Was it . . . was before . . . he was before the social programs from the standpoint of . . . he was for standing up for Roe v. Wade before he was against first . . . Roe v. Wade?"

———

*Herman Cain on the different flavors of ice cream to which he'd compare his primary competitors, November 2011:* Michele Bachmann? I'm not going to say it. I'm not going to say it. Tutti-frutti I know I'm going to get in trouble!"

———

*Donald Trump, flinging water from a water bottle at a rally, February 26, 2016:* "Have you ever seen a guy sweat like this?! It's Rubio!"

———

*Donald Trump, speaking about one-time presidential candidate Pat Buchanan, October 25, 1999:* "He's a Hitler-lover. I guess he's an anti-Semite. He doesn't like the blacks, he doesn't like the gays. It's just incredible that anyone can embrace this guy. And maybe he'll get 4 or 5 percent of the vote and it'll be a really staunch right, wacko vote."

———

*Donald Trump, at the Family Leadership Discussion in Ames, Iowa, on July 18, 2015, talking about Senator and former POW John McCain:* "He's not a war hero. He was a war hero because he was captured. I like people who weren't captured."

———

*Donald Trump, Twitter, February 11, 2016:* Remember, it was the Republican Party, with the help of Conservatives, that made so many promises to their base, BUT DIDN'T KEEP THEM!"

### Famously, Richard Nixon is "Not a crook":

"People have got to know whether or not their president is a crook. Well, I'm not a crook. I've earned everything I've got." *(at a news conference, November 17, 1973)*

———

"When the President does it, that means it's not illegal." *(in a 1977 interview with David Frost)*

### I see some noses growing:

"I haven't had a gaffe." *(Michele Bachmann, November 18, 2011)*

———

*When being questioned on June 11, 2007, Sen. Larry Craig explained to his arresting officer why his foot was in two stalls (a sign of soliciting prostitution):* "[I have] a wide stance."

*About his diaries, where he bragged about sexual encounters he had with staff members, Sen. Bob Packwood wrote:* "A number of things that I put in [the diary] were inaccurate, and some of them simply weren't true. On occasion, I discovered I would recount conversations that simply didn't happen." *(September 11, 1995)*

### On running:

*Donald Trump, GOP debate, August 6, 2015:* "I can't say that I have to respect that person who wins. . . . If I'm the nominee, I pledge I will not run as an independent." *(But of course you're not running as an independent if you're the nominee!)*

### Trump's reaction to John Boehner not being Speaker of the House anymore:

"I don't like the crying." *(March 16, 2011, ABC News)*

### On Obama:

*Donald Trump, Twitter, September 10, 2014:* "If Obama resigns from office NOW, thereby doing a great service to the country—I will give him free lifetime golf at any one of my courses!"

*Trump, at a Tea Party rally in Boca Raton, Florida, April 2011, after reading books by Obama:* "The man that wrote the second book . . . didn't write the first book. The difference was like chicken salad and chicken shit."

*Mostly, Obama refers to Islamic terrorist groups by their names, such as Al Qaeda or ISIS/ISIL. Bobby Jindal's opinion on that, Fox News,*

*June 25, 2015:* "As president I would actually name the enemy, radical Islamic terrorists. We've got a president who wants to apologize for America and wants to criticize medieval Christian and wants to wage war on junk food. He won't even say the words 'radical Islamic terrorists.'"

———

*Donald Trump, in 2011, three weeks before Obama released his long-form birth certificate:* "I would like to have him show his birth certificate, and can I be honest with you, I hope he can. Because if he can't, if he can't, if he wasn't born in this country, which is a real possibility . . . then he has pulled one of the great cons in the history of politics."

———

*Mike Huckabee, December 1, 2015, in a Fox News op-ed called "America Needs a Commander-in-Chief, Not an Obsessed Meteorologist":* "Maybe [President Obama] would take ISIS seriously if he discovered they didn't recycle."

———

*To Mike Huckabee, Obama's birth certificate wasn't enough:* "Let him make this challenge: I'll release my tax returns when Barack Obama releases his college transcripts and the copy of his admission records to show whether he got any loans as a foreign student. When he releases that, talk to me about my tax returns." *(The O'Reilly Factor, January 20, 2012)*

### John McCain, on why he picked Sarah Palin as his running mate:
"I think she's most qualified of any that has run recently for vice president, tell you the truth." *(Interview with Don Imus, October 2008)*

*Mike Huckabee settled the mock-dispute between Conan O'Brien, Stephen Colbert, and Jon Stewart over who "made" him, via satellite on* The Late Show:

"Let's be clear: None of these guys made me. This great nation made me. So vote for me. God bless America and forget these three idiots." *(January 17, 2008)*


*On September 6, 2005, Sen. Rick Santorum (R-PA), suggested that Katrina victims should be punished if they didn't evacuate New Orleans:*

"I mean, you have people who don't heed those warnings and then put people at risk as a result of not heeding those warnings. . . . There may be a need to look at tougher penalties on those who decide to ride it out and understand that there are consequences to not leaving."


*On sticking it to The Man: Steve King protesting the change to energy-efficient lightbulbs:*

"And at night, the janitors would come through, which were Nancy's Stasi troops, and screw out those light bulbs, those Edison bulbs, and give me, every once in a while, those curlicue bulbs. . . . So I got this green bag right here. And I filled it up with the black market light bulbs. And I brought them back to my office here in the Capitol. Whenever I need to put a bulb in the lamp, I reach in this green bag and I screw it in there and smile. A little bit of my liberty back. A little bit of our freedom back. And I want to challenge you to do the same thing. Bring back some of that liberty, some of that freedom." *(CPAC, Washington DC, February 9, 2012)*

***Steve King, justifying leaving anti-dogfighting legislation at a tele-town hall meeting on July 31, 2012, by comparing it to . . . wrestling?!:***

When the legislation that passed in the farm bill that says that it's a federal crime to watch animals fight or to induce someone else to watch an animal fight, but it's not a federal crime to induce somebody to watch people fighting, there's something wrong with the priorities of people that think like that.

### On running for senate:

*Mike Huckabee:* "There's a greater chance that I would dye my hair green and get tattoos all over my body and do a rock tour with Amy Winehouse than there is that I would run for the Senate, so let me put that to rest." *(February 12, 2008)*

***Jeb Bush, on making Americans work more (when speaking with New Hampshire's union leader in July 2015):***

"My aspiration for the country and I believe we can achieve it, is 4 percent growth as far as the eye can see . . . which means we have to be a lot more productive, workforce participation has to rise from its all-time modern lows. It means that people need to work longer hours."

***Rand Paul, on changes CNBC proposed to their Republican presidential debate:***

"If we don't have opening and closing statements, CNBC can go f**k themselves." *(October 2015)*

### On spending:

"We spend more money on antacids than we do on politics." *(John Boehner, on Sunday, May 3, 2015, in comments on NBC's Meet the Press)*

## On false equivalencies:

"The world is starving for American leadership. But America has an antiwar president." *(John Boehner, March 23, 2015)*

## When Donald Trump claimed he had superpowers?:

"My Twitter has become so powerful that I can make my enemies tell the truth." *(Twitter, October 17, 2012)*

## Rep. Marlin Stutzman (R-IN), on the benefits of a government shutdown:

"We're not going to be disrespected. We have to get something out of this. And I don't know what that even is." *(October 1, 2013)*

## Michele Bachmann believes Obama expanding AmeriCorps leads to re-education camps?:

"The real concern is that there are provisions for what I would call re-education camps for young people, where young people have to go and get trained in a philosophy that the government puts forward and then they have to go to work in some of these politically correct forums." *(April 6, 2009, interview with radio host Sue Jeffers)*

## Rick Perry, experiencing an onstage meltdown during a 2011 GOP debate, forgetting about his plan to cut the Department of Energy, and what the three branches of government are:

"I will tell you: it's three agencies of government, when I get there, that are gone: Commerce, Education and the . . . what's the third one there? Let's see. . . . OK. So Commerce, Education and the . . . The third agency of government I would . . . I would do away with the Education, the . . . Commerce and . . . let's see . . . I can't. The third one, I can't. Sorry. Oops."

**James Watt, former Secretary of State, on diversity, September 1983:**

"We have every mixture you can have. I have a black, a woman, two Jews, and a cripple. And we have talent."

**In this widely published quote, George Bush Sr. tries to talk to a group of students about drug abuse:**

"Now, like, I'm president. It would be pretty hard for some drug guy to come into the White House and start offering it up, you know? . . . I bet if they did, I hope I would say, 'Hey, get lost. We don't want any of that.'"

**Newt Gingrich, speaking at the 1996 Republican convention, on how beach volleyball sticks it to The Man:**

"A mere forty years ago, beach volleyball was just beginning. No bureaucrat would have invented it, and that's what freedom is all about."

**Donald Trump, on losing the Iowa Caucuses:**

"Because I was told I could not do well in Iowa, I spent very little there—a fraction of Cruz and Rubio. Came in a strong second. Great honor." *(February 2, 2016, after coming in second to Ted Cruz. The next day, Trump shared on Twitter:* "Ted Cruz didn't win Iowa, he stole it. That is why all of the polls were so wrong and why he got far more votes than anticipated. Bad!"*)*

**Must be a magic gavel:**

"The thing is, if you control the Senate meetings, you control the gavel. And the gavel is a very important instrument . . . an instrument of power. An instrument that establishes the agenda." *(widely attributed to Dan Quayle)*

### An American about America:

"I believe in an America where millions of Americans believe in an America that's the America millions of Americans believe in. That's the America I love." (*Mitt Romney, January 2012 stump speech, quoted in* National Review)

---

*At the February 25, 2016, GOP debate, when asked how he would pick a nominee for SCOTUS, Ben Carson replied:* "The fruit salad of their life is what I would look at."

### On constituents:

*Republican National Committee Chairman Michael Steele, announcing another run for chairmanship, let this slip in December 2010:* "We need to uptick our image with everyone, including one-armed midgets."

---

*At the Daytona 500 in 2012, Mitt Romney, admired NASCAR fans' plastic ponchos:* "I like those fancy raincoats you bought. Really sprung for the big bucks."

### Arnold on FIAH!!!:

*When asked what his favorite color was, Arnold Schwarzenegger once replied:* "I like the color red because it's a fire. And I see myself as always being on fire."

### Squishes:

*When Ted Cruz threatened to filibuster gun control legislation that several (angry) Republican senators wanted passed, he had this to say:* "They said, 'Listen, before you did this the politics of this were great—the Dems were the bad guys, the Republicans were the good guys. Now we all look like a bunch of squishes.' Well, there is an alternative—you could just not be a bunch of squishes." *(April 26, 2013, FreedomWorks Summit)*

### View from the Martian Canals:

*After winning his state's GOP Senate nomination, August 5, 2013, Ted Cruz laid down his views on reaching across the aisle (and the solar system) via* Fox News Sunday: "I am perfectly happy to compromise and work with anybody. Republicans, Democrats, Libertarians. I'll work with Martians. If—and the 'if' is critical—they're willing to cut spending and reduce the debt."

### Fair weather oranges:

*When visiting California, Bob Dole said this about their oranges on March 25, 1996:* "I know there are California oranges and Florida oranges. When I'm in Florida, I like Florida oranges. Today, I think California oranges are the best, of course."

### On violent videogames:

*Lamar Alexander (R-TN), January 30, 2013, Senate Judiciary Committee Hearing:* "You know, I think video games is a bigger problems than guns because video games affect people, but the First Amendment limits what we can do about video games."

———

*Mike Johanns (R-NE), April 19, 2013, US Senate floor:* "Apparently we should ban these devices in rural Nebraska, where we grew up around firearms, but allow our children to idolize Hollywood stars committing mass shootings on the big screen, and then try it out for yourself in a graphic video game where the game is interactive, violent, and you are literally shooting at people."

———————

*In response to the Columbine massacre, a lot of politicians blamed rock music and video games for the shooting. Newt Gingrich was apparently one of them:* "And let us say to Hollywood, and let us say to the Nintendos and the other games, if you are going to be sick, we are going to find a way to protect this country from you." *(Congressional hearing, June 29, 1999)*

### Visions of the future:

*President Ronald Reagan told reporters as he arrived at the GOP convention in 1979:* "I had a dream the other night. I dreamed that Jimmy Carter came to me and asked why I wanted his job. I told him I didn't want his job. I want to be president."

### OCTOPUS TEETH?!:

*On the Pure Opelka podcast on June 21, 2014, when Ted Cruz was asked to tell the audience a surprising fact about himself, he said:* "I was bitten by an octopus."

### Ted Cruz, designated driver:

*At the third GOP debate at the University of Colorado–Boulder, October 25, 2015, when asked about critics, he went on a rant about anti-Republican bias, including the quote:* "If you want someone to grab a beer with, I may not be that guy. But if you want someone to drive you home, I'll get the job done." *(When moderator Carl Quintanilla told him his time was up and mentioned that he didn't deliver on the beer, Cruz quipped:* "I'll buy you some tequila, or some famous Colorado brownies.")

## Scaring little girls:

*Giving a speech in New Hampshire on March 15, 2015, Ted Cruz told the crowd:* "With the Obama-Clinton foreign policy of leading from behind—the whole world is on fire." *(When a little girl behind him asked:* "The world is on fire?" *Cruz responded:* "Yes! Your world is on fire!")

## Puppies make everything better, according to Dan Quayle:

"The other day the president said, I know you've had some rough times, and I want to do something that will show the nation what faith that I have in you, in your maturity and sense of responsibility. He paused, then said, would you like a puppy?" *(From the* Los Angeles Times, *May 16, 1989)*

## Your meter time is up:

*After being asked repeatedly on April 20, 1989, whether he will launch an investigation into the Iran-Contra Affair, former president George H. W. Bush snapped:* "Please don't ask me to do that which I've just said I'm not going to do, because you're burning up time. The meter is running through the sand on you, and I am now filibustering."

## Bob Dole (R-KS) on the senate floor, thinking he was in a science-fiction scene:

"Merely presenting a driver's license or other document based on a birth certificate is not enough for an accurate verification. Biometric verification of identity must be made and then a database of those persons who have legal status must be checked." *(October 21, 1988)*

*Vice President Dan Quayle, enjoying a view from the Martian Canals:*

"Mars is essentially in the same orbit. . . . Mars is somewhat the same distance from the Sun, which is very important. We have seen pictures where there are canals, we believe, and water. If there is water, that means there is oxygen. If oxygen, that means we can breathe." *(August 11, 1989)*

*Mitt Romney, suggesting it would be a good idea to crack a window in a pressurized cabin at 35,000 feet with 500-mile-an-hour winds:*

"When you have a fire in an aircraft, there's no place to go, exactly, there's no . . . and you can't find any oxygen from outside the aircraft to get in the aircraft, because the windows don't open. I don't know why they don't do that. It's a real problem." *(Beverly Hills fund-raiser, September 22, 2012)*

*Rep. Lamar Smith (R-TX), on the media:*

"The greatest threat to America is not necessarily a recession or even another terrorist attack. The greatest threat to America is a liberal media bias." *(June 4, 2009)*

*Bobby Jindal, on margins:*

"When the front-runners are still clumped together around 10 percent, what that tells me there is a path wide open for folks. I get the sense that voters are saying this isn't about just one good impression." *(Wall Street Journal, June 24, 2015)*

*Michele Bachmann, speaking about the Declaration of Independence—which did not end slavery:*

"The very founders that wrote those documents worked tirelessly until slavery was no more in the United States. And I think it is high time that we recognize the contribution of our forebears, who worked tirelessly, men like John Quincy Adams, who would not rest until slavery was extinguished in the country." *(speaking before the Iowans for Tax Relief, January 21, 2011)*

**Rick Perry, on the number of justices in SCOTUS (he's right until we get another one, but when he made the statement, there were nine):**

"I trust those independent school districts to make those decisions better than eight unelected and, frankly, unaccountable judges." *(December 9, 2011, interview with the* Des Moines Register*)*

**Perry, flubbing the voting age (which has been 18 since 1971), as well as the date of the November 6 election:**

"Those of you that will be 21 by November the 12th, I ask for your support and your vote." *(speaking at Saint Anselm in Manchester, New Hampshire, November 27, 2011)*

**On being a time traveler (apparently):**

"The Holocaust was an obscene period in our nation's history. I mean in this century's history. But I didn't live in this century." *(Vice President Dan Quayle, September 15, 1988)*

**Misquoting/misremembering:**

*On Twitter, May 14, 2015, Scott Walker, governor of Wisconsin, misquoted Thomas Jefferson:* "Thomas Jefferson said it best . . . that government is best which governs least." *(Henry David Thoreau actually wrote this in* Civil Disobedience.*)*

---

*Jody Hice, with another quote Jefferson never said:* "Most Bad Government has grown out of Too Much Government." *(Facebook, January 24, 2014)*

*Hey, Rand Paul (R-KY), Patrick Henry never said this:* "Patrick Henry said this, Patrick Henry said the Constitution is about 'restraining the government not the people—lest it come to dominate our lives and interests.'" *(Greenville, South Carolina, June 1, 2015)*

---

*Ben Carson, misquoting Alexis de Tocqueville, in the CPAC leaflet, published 2015:* "He concluded his American analysis by saying, 'America is great, because America is good. If America ever ceases to be good, she will cease to be great.'"

---

*Ben Carson, misquoting Stalin during the February 13, 2016, GOP debate:* "Joseph Stalin said if you want to bring America down you have to undermine three things: our spiritual life, our patriotism, and our morality."

---

*Ronald Reagan, at the 1988 Republican National Convention, attempting to quote John Adams, who actually said, "Facts are stubborn things," not: "Facts are stupid things."*

## L'etat c'est-moi!:

*When former house majority leader Tom DeLay was told to put out his cigar by the owner of Ruth's Chris Steak House on May 14, 2003, due to federal government regulations banning smoking in buildings, he roared:* "I AM the federal government."

## Ted Cruz, January 2014, talking about a government shutdown he proposed the previous September:

"I think it was a mistake that President Obama and the Democrats shut the government down this fall."

**Rick Perry, incorrectly stating that the American Revolution occurred during the 1500s:**

"Our Founding Fathers never meant for Washington DC to be the fount of all wisdom. As a matter of fact they were very much afraid of that because they'd just had this experience with this far-away government that had centralized thought process and planning and what have you, and then it was actually the reason that we fought the revolution in the sixteenth century was to get away from that kind of onerous crown if you will." *(October 12, 2011, answering questions from students at Dartmouth University after the GOP debate)*

**Ron Johnson (R-WI), on Photoshop:**

*At a Senate Foreign Relations Committee hearing, July 23, 2015, asserting that a photo-shopped image of Obama and Rouhani (they never met) was real:* "I don't know what you're talking about. You're saying that's a photoshop—can you explain what you're talking about?"

**Herman Cain, explaining his "We need a leader, not a reader," Tweet, November 2011:**

"Engage the people. Don't try to pass a 2,700-page bill—and even they didn't read it! You and I didn't have time to read it. We're too busy trying to live—send our kids to school. That's why I am only going to allow small bills—three pages."

**Some Quayle-isms (via Dan Quayle, vice president from 1989 to 1993):**

*December 6, 1989:* "One word sums up probably the responsibility of any vice president, and that one word is 'to be prepared.'"

---

Sh*t Politicians Say

*The Quayles' (misspelled) 1989 Christmas card:* "May our nation continue to be the beakon of hope to the world."

———

*Speech to California delegates to the Republican National Convention, August 17, 1988:* "Let me just tell you how thrilling it really is, and how, what a challenge it is, because in 1988 the question is whether we're going forward to tomorrow or whether we're going to go past to the back! . . . That's a Hoosierism. You've got to get used to that!"

———

*Riffing on the organization's slogan "A mind is a terrible thing to waste," Dan got it all wrong in a May 1989 address to the United Negro College Fund:* "What a waste it is to lose one's mind. Or not to have a mind is being very wasteful. How true that is."

———

*Oh, the unfortunate event of working with the Bushes:* "It is not just age; it's accomplishments, it's experience. I have far more experience than many others that sought the office of vice president of this country. I have as much experience in the Congress as Jack Kennedy did when he sought the presidency. I will be prepared to deal with the people in the Bush administration, if that unfortunate event would ever occur." *(Vice-presidential candidates' debate, October 5, 1988)*

## Herman Cain, apparently unaware that presidents do not sign constitutional amendments:

"Yes. Yes I feel that strongly about it. If we can get the necessary support and it comes to my desk I'll sign it. That's all I can do. I will sign it." *(In an interview David Brody on Christian Broadcast Network, October 22, 2011)*

**Ted Cruz, on the Internet:**

"'Net Neutrality'" is Obamacare for the Internet; the Internet should not operate at the speed of government." *(Twitter, November 10, 2014)*

**Dan Coats (R-IN), after he sat there listening to a hearing and being surprised that the subject matter was not what he expected it to be. A staffer saw him at the meeting and let him know why:**

"I just got a note saying I'm at the wrong hearing." *(April 3, 2013, Washington DC)*

**Herman Cain, speaking in a state with a lot of Spanish speakers:**

"How do you say 'delicious' in Cuban?" *(Campaign stop in Florida, November 17, 2011)*

**Ted Cruz's sarcastic remarks at a Tea Party event in Houston, Texas:**

"I've spent the past month in Washington DC and it is terrific to be back in America." *(Reported in* Washington Examiner, *Oct. 22, 2013)*

**Harvard-educated Mitt Romney rips into Obama at a campaign stop in Harrisburg, Pennsylvania:**

"We have a president, who I think is a nice guy, but he spent too much time at Harvard, perhaps." *(April 5, 2012)*

**What happened to 9/11:**

*Rudy Giuliani forgetting about 9/11 (he was mayor of NYC when it happened):* "We had no domestic attacks under Bush; we've had one under Obama." *(January 8, 2010, on* Good Morning America*)*

### On his Republican rivals:

*Ben Carson, top neurosurgeon:* "(I'm) the only one to take out half a brain, although you would think, if you go to Washington, that someone had beat me to it." *(First GOP debate, Cleveland, August 6, 2015)*

### Things going bump in the night:

*Herbert Hoover, addressing the John Marshall Republican Club, St. Louis:* "A good many things creep around in the dark besides Santa Claus." *(December 16, 1935)*

### GOP presidential candidate Herman Cain, quoting lyrics from a disco queen in his 2011 concession speech:

"A poet once said, 'Life can be a challenge, life can seem impossible, but it's never easy when there's so much on the line.'" *(The "poetry" he's referring to was sung by Donna Summer. It's the theme song to* Pokémon: The Movie 2000. *Fortunately, Cain said the words—he didn't sing them.)*

### John Boehner, on Congress (appears true though, especially now):

"But, you know, I'm presiding over an institution that was designed not to work." *(Interview with Judy Woodruff, February 4, 2012)*

### Bobby Jindal, on Common Core:

*In an op-ed for USA Today, after endorsing Common Core in his state in 2009:* "I'm from the school that believes education is a matter best left for local control. The notion of Washington determining curricula is something most states are simply not interested in. It's a non-starter." *(Note: CC was a state-led initiative.)*

---

*On Fox News, six years later:* "Look at the math, it makes absolutely no sense to a lot of our kids, including my own children." *(June 18, 2015)*

### Ben Carson, on being shot:

*On October 6, 2015, Carson recalled this incident:* "A guy comes in and puts a gun in my ribs. And I just said, 'I believe that you want the guy behind the counter.'" *(Two days later, on* Fox & Friends, *he made this statement about what he would do if he were at the massacre in Oregon that happened the day before and confronted by the gunman* "Not only would I probably not cooperate with him, I would not just stand there and let him shoot me, I would say, 'Hey guys, everybody attack him. He may shoot me, but he can't get us all.'")*

### Mitt Romney, on Hugo Chavez, leader of Venezuela, March 9, 2011:

"Hugo Chavez has tried to steal an inspiring phrase 'Patria o muerte, venceremos.' It does not belong to him. It belongs to a free Cuba." *(Note: Romney invoked a phrase that translates to "Fatherland or death, we shall overcome," which Fidel Castro has used to close his speeches for years.)*

### Dan Quayle, spelling champ:

"Add one little bit on the end. . . . Think of 'potato,' how's it spelled? You're right phonetically, but what else . . . ? There ya go . . . all right!" *(Famously "correcting" a student's already correct spelling of the word "potato" during a spelling bee at an elementary school, Trenton, New Jersey, June 17, 1992)*

### Mitt Romney, on borders, during the third presidential debate:

"Syria is Iran's only ally in the Arab world. It's their route to the sea." *(October 22, 2012. Note: Iran and Syria do not share a border, as they're separated by Iraq.)*

### College-educated Rick Santorum:

"President Obama wants everybody in America to go to college. What a snob . . . Oh, I understand why he wants you to go to college. He wants to remake you in his image." *(At a campaign stop in Michigan, February 25, 2012)*

### Republican presidential candidate Herman Cain, warning that China could develop nuclear weapons:

"They [China] have indicated that they're trying to develop nuclear capability and they want to develop more aircraft carriers like we have. So yes, we have to consider them a military threat." *(Interview with Judy Woodruff, November 1, 2011. Note: China has had nukes since 1964.)*

### Harvard Law School graduate Ted Cruz:

"Sequestration sounds like an exotic wildlife disease. Nobody has any idea what the heck that is." *(Washington Examiner, October 24, 2013)*

### Ted Cruz, on gluten-free food in the military:

"That's why the last thing any commander should need to worry about is the grades he is getting from some plush-bottomed Pentagon bureaucrat for political correctness or social experiments or providing gluten-free MREs." *(Aboard the USS Yorktown, South Carolina, February 16, 2016)*

### House Majority Leader Tom DeLay (R-TX), to three young hurricane evacuees from New Orleans, seeking shelter in the Houston Astrodome:

"Now tell me the truth boys, is this kind of fun?" *(September 9, 2005)*

***Mitt Romney, supporting state initiatives (specifically about the antiunion law ballot initiative in Ohio):***

"I'm not saying anything one way or the other about the two ballot issues. I am not speaking about the particular ballot issues. Those are up to the people of Ohio. But I certainly support the efforts of the governor to reign in the scale of government. I am not terribly familiar with the two ballot initiatives. But I am certainly supportive of the Republican Party's efforts here." *(During a campaign stop in Cincinnati, Ohio. October 25, 2011)*

---

"I fully support Governor Kasich's . . . I think it's called 'Question 2' in Ohio. Fully support that. In fact, on my website as far back as April I laid out I supported 'Question 2.' . . . I support it 110 percent." *(now, apparently fully supporting the Ohio antiunion law during an event in Fairfax, Virginia, October 26, 2011)*

***Calvin Coolidge, on the Presidency (that explains a lot):***

"I think the American Public want a solemn ass as a president. And I think I'll go along with them." *(to Ethel Barrymore, 1924)*

***Ronald Reagan, on Vietnam veterans and their rights:***

"Because Vietnam was not a declared war, the veterans are not even eligible for the G. I. Bill of Rights with respect to education or anything." *(Newsweek, April 21, 1980)*

***Mitch McConnell, on appointing someone to SCOTUS (or, when the shoe's on the other foot):***

"My view is that the president won the election, no matter what the margin, and is entitled to tilt the judiciary in the direction that he feels appropriate." *(2001, after George W. Bush won the electoral vote as decided by the Supreme Court in* Bush v. Gore*)*

---

"The American people should have a voice in the selection of their next Supreme Court justice. This vacancy should not be filled until we have a new president." *(2016, after Scalia's death, when it falls on Obama to appoint someone to the bench)*

### Republicans are bad at prognosticating:

*Ronald Reagan (then a candidate for governor of California):* "It's silly talking about how many years we will have to spend in the jungles of Vietnam when we could pave the whole country and put parking stripes on it and still be home by Christmas." *(interviewed in the* Fresno Bee*, October 10, 1965)*

---

Dr. Julius Klein, assistant secretary of commerce: "The Depression has ended. . . . In July, up we go." *(June 9, 1931. The Depression would last another decade.)*

---

Herbert Hoover, address at the annual dinner with the Chamber of Commerce: "While the crash only took place six months ago, I am convinced we have now passed the worst and with continued unity of effort we shall rapidly recover. There is one certainty of the future of a people of the resources, intelligence and character of the people of the United States—that is, prosperity." *(May 1, 1930)*

### Richard Nixon, on Watergate:

"I was under medication when I made the decision to burn the tapes." *(1973)*

---

"You know, I've always wondered about the taping equipment. But I'm damn glad we have it." *(to White House Chief of Staff H. R. Haldeman)*

### What did you expect?:

"Wherever I have gone in this country, I have found Americans." *(Alf Landon, in a campaign speech while running against FDR in 1936)*

### And finally, Ted Cruz, demonstrating "recycling":

"I've rolled out a detailed plan to cut $500 billion in federal spending, specifying exactly what I would cut easy to say it, but one of the great disconnects to all of the people, all of the voters. I understand the folks who are supporting Donald right now. You're angry. You're angry at Washington, and he uses angry rhetoric . . ." *(He says all this as he eats a booger (some say it was a tonsil stone, others say it was used food that came up, I just say ew!) that rolled from his nose to his mouth at the GOP debate, March 3, 2016.)*

# Chapter 5

## Sh*t Politicians Say About Money and the Economy

I think I speak for everyone when I say that we've been in the toilet as far as money's concerned. Some of us are still there. But instead of using common sense solutions to fix the problem, politicians waste their time (and ours) opening their mouths and saying *stupid* shit. *Most of their spewed garbage is to placate their buddies on Wall Street, something I loathe, and while some of it is just being ignorant, in the end, it's all stupid.*

### Back in the 1950s, the top tax rate was 90 percent. I wonder if Ronald Reagan thought that decade was a "time of lawlessness":

"History shows that when the taxes of a nation approach about 20 percent of the people's income, there begins to be a lack of respect for government. . . . When it reaches 25 percent, there comes an increase in lawlessness." (Time *magazine, April 14, 1980)*

### Newt Gingrich, on capitalism:

"The idea that a congressman would be tainted by accepting money from private industry or private sources is essentially a socialist argument." (Mother Jones *magazine, October 1989)*

*Former speaker of the house Nancy Pelosi, trying to drum up support for the economic stimulus bill (which leaves me wondering: how many of the 300 million Americans would have to lose their jobs twice if this thing didn't pass):*

"Every month that we do not have an economic recovery package 500 million Americans lose their jobs." *(October 2008)*

### Mitt Romney, on job creation:

*Flip:* "As president, I will create 12 million new jobs." *(second presidential debate, October 16, 2012)*

---

*Flop:* "Government does not create jobs. Government does not create jobs." *(45 minutes later, same debate)*

### On the national debt:

*Pete Stark, interview with Jan Helfeld, 2008:* "The national debt measures the wealth . . . the wealthier we are . . . the national debt . . . it's an indication of the wealth of the country."

### Mike Huckabee, on the federal budget:

It's the best proposal that we ought to have because it's flatter, it's fairer, it's finite, it's family friendly. And instead, we've had a Congress that spent money like John Edwards at a beauty shop. *(Republican presidential candidate debate, Johnston, Iowa, December 12, 2007)*

### Mike Huckabee, on funding welfare:

*About a bipartisan effort to block new limits for welfare recipients:* "People need to remember that to balance the federal budget off the backs of the poorest people in the country is simply unacceptable. You don't pull feeding tubes from people. You don't pull the wheelchair out from under the child with muscular dystrophy." *(December 26, 2004, to the* New York Times*)*

---

*Proposing his "Fair Tax" at the GOP debate:* "The money paid at consumption is paid by everybody, including illegals, prostitutes, pimps, drug dealers, and anyone living off the government." *(August 7, 2015)*

### On making a lot of money:

*Barack Obama on Wall Street Reform:* "We're not trying to push financial reform because we begrudge success that's fairly earned. I mean, I do think at a certain point you've made enough money. But, you know, part of the American way is, you know, you can just keep on making it if you're providing a good product or providing good service. We don't want people to stop, ah, fulfilling the core responsibilities of the financial system to help grow our economy." *(Quincy, Illinois, April 29, 2010)*

---

*Ted Cruz, about Donald Trump:* "Listen, we can all understand if you write a check to a city commissioner, for a zoning waiver on building a building. It may be corrupt, but you can understand." *(at the GOP debate, Detroit, March 3, 2016)*

### Rick Perry, referring to Social Security as a Ponzi scheme despite the fact that it pays people back more money than they pay in:

"The Republican candidates are talking about ways to transition this program and it is a monstrous lie. It is a Ponzi scheme to tell our kids that are 25 or 30 years old today that you're paying into a program that's going to be there. Anybody that's for the status quo with Social Security today is involved with a monstrous lie to our kids, and it's not right." *(GOP presidential debate, September 14, 2011)*

### Mitch McConnell flip-flop on Citizens United and Super PACs:

*Flips:*

"What we ought to do is eliminate the political action committee contributions, because those are the ones that raise the specter of undue influence. And those can be gone tomorrow. We can pass a bill tomorrow to take care of that problem." *(1987)*

––––––––––

"We Republicans have put together a responsible and constitutional campaign reform agenda. It would restrict the power of special-interest PACS, stop the flow of all soft money, keep wealthy individuals from buying public office." *(1988)*

––––––––––

*Flops:*

*McConnell to the Koch Brothers, who formed a Super PAC to help McConnell's political goals:* "I want to start by thanking you, Charles and David, for the important work you're doing, I don't know where I'd be without you." *(2014)*

––––––––––

"All *Citizens United* did was to level the playing field for corporate speech. We now have, I think, the most free and open system we've had in modern times." *(2014)*

### Michele Bachmann, overestimating the cost of presidential trips (note, the record for the most expensive trip taken by any president goes to Bill Clinton, at a cost of $10 million a day):

"The president of the United States will be taking a trip over to India that is expected to cost the taxpayers $200 million a day. He's taking 2,000 people with him. He will be renting out over 870 rooms in India. And these are five-star hotel rooms at the

Taj Mahal Palace Hotel. This is the kind of over-the-top spending." *(November 3, 2010, CNN interview)*

### GOP presidential candidate Mitt Romney, on Citizens United:

"Corporations are people, my friend . . . of course they are. Everything corporations earn ultimately goes to the people. Where do you think it goes? Whose pockets? Whose pockets? People's pockets. Human beings, my friend." *(August 11, 2011, at a campaign stop at the Iowa State Fair in Des Moines. Apparently, people didn't believe him, as the line drew boos from the crowd!)*

### Cynthia Davis (R-MO), on free lunch, arguing against school lunch programs which continue into the summer:

"Hunger can be a positive motivator." *(June 16, 2009, in her newsletter)*

### Obama's campaign, on Super PACs:

*Flip:* "Neither the president nor his campaign staff or aides will fund-raise for super PACs." *(Obama's campaign spokesman Ben LaBolt, July 9, 2011)*

---

*Flop:* "Senior campaign officials as well as some White House and Cabinet officials will attend and speak at [super PAC] Priorities USA fund-raising events." (Obama's campaign manager Jim Messina, February 6, 2012)

### Hillary Clinton, on the Trans-Pacific Partnership, 2012:

"We need to keep upping our game both bilaterally and with partners across the region through agreements like the Trans-Pacific Partnership or TPP. This TPP sets the gold standard in trade agreements to open free, transparent, fair trade, the kind of environment that has the rule of law and a level playing field. And when negotiated, this agreement will cover 40 percent of the world's total trade and build in strong protections for workers and the environment." *(Later, in 2016, she said during the Democratic debates that she would "reserve judgment until a final deal was made.")*

### . . . And on NAFTA:

*Flip:* "I think everybody is in favor of free and fair trade. I think NAFTA is proving its worth." *(Hillary Clinton, 1996)*

––––––––––

*Flop:* "Creating a free trade zone in North America—the largest free trade zone in the world—would expand US exports, create jobs and ensure that our economy was reaping the benefits, not the burdens, of globalization. Although unpopular with labor unions, expanding trade opportunities was an important administration goal." *(2003, in her memoir)*

––––––––––

*Flop (or is it a flip?!):* "NAFTA was a mistake to the extent that it did not deliver on what we had hoped it would, and that's why I call for a trade timeout." *(Hillary Clinton, speaking during the presidential debate on CNN, November 2007)*

### Ted Cruz, on financial boogeyman Obama:

"'We'll never default on the debt' and the reason the president isn't doing that is he's trying to scare people and raise the specter of financial apocalypse." *(Fox News Sunday, January 6, 2012)*

### Mitt Romney, on bailing out Ford:

*Flip:* "If General Motors, Ford, and Chrysler get the bailout that their chief executives asked for yesterday, you can kiss the

American automotive industry goodbye." *(2008* New York Times *op-ed titled "Let Detroit Go Bankrupt")*

---

*Flop:* "I pushed the idea of a managed bankruptcy. And finally, when that was done, and help was given, the companies got back on their feet. So I'll take a lot of credit for the fact that this industry's come back." (*Speaking about the US auto industry's comeback, in an interview with WEWS Cleveland, 2012*)

## Romney, on trust funds:

*Flip: Challenging Ted Kennedy about his family's trusts during the Massachusetts Senate race:* "The blind trust is an age-old ruse, if you will, which is to say, you can always tell the blind trust what it can and cannot do. You give a blind trust rules." *(October 18, 1994)*

---

*Flop: Responding the criticism from Democrats about his alleged offshore accounts:* "I don't manage the money that I have. In order to make sure that I didn't have a conflict of interest while I was governor or while I was considering a run for national office, I had a blind trust established." *(2012)*

## Charles Rangel, on voting for Social Security, October 29, 2013:

"It should give you some small comfort to know that, historically, the Republican Party always fought vigorously against these type of programs. I don't think that one Republican voted for the Social Security Act, even though those old enough enjoy the benefits." *(A quick Google search can tell you that plenty of Republicans supported Social Security in 1935, when it was proposed, both in the House and the Senate, and there were Democrats who opposed it in both the Senate and the House.)*

**Rick Santorum, on how Social Security doesn't work:**

"The reason Social Security is in big trouble is we don't have enough workers to support the retirees. Well, a third of all the young people in America are not in America today because of abortion." *(during a Republican presidential debate, May 2011)*

**Herman Cain, on the poor, said in response to Occupy protesters:**

"Don't blame Wall Street, don't blame the big banks, if you don't have a job and you're not rich, blame yourself!" *(*Wall Street Journal, *October 5, 2011)*

**On welfare:**

*Former house majority leader Tom DeLay, interview with CNN, March 7, 2010:* "There is an argument to be made that these extensions, the unemployment benefits, keep people from going and finding job. In fact there are some studies that have been done that show people stay on unemployment compensation and they don't look for a job until two or three weeks before they know the benefits are going to run out.

CNN's CANDY CROWLEY: "People are unemployed because they want to be?

TOM DELAY: "Well, it is the truth. And people in the real world know it."

*South Carolina Lt. Governor Andre Bauer, speaking against free and reduced school lunches during a town hall meeting:* "My grandmother was not a highly educated woman, but she told me as a small child to quit feeding stray animals. You know why? Because they breed. You're facilitating the problem if you give an animal or a person ample food supply. They will reproduce, especially ones that don't think too much further than that. And so what you've got to do is you've got to curtail that type of behavior.

Sh*t Politicians Say

They don't know any better." *(Reported by the* Greenfield News, *January 2010. He later said that* "maybe the stray animals wasn't the best metaphor.")

---

*Michele Bachmann, saying in an interview with Tom DeLay that the unemployed should starve, reiterating a line she made at a speech for the Family Research Council (FRC):* "Our nation needs to stop doing for people what they can and should do for themselves. Self-reliance means, if anyone will not work, neither should he eat." *(November 2011)*

### Barack Obama, on raising the debt ceiling:

*Flip: As a freshman senator, in March 2006, during discussions on raising the debt ceiling before votes were cast:* "America has a debt problem and a failure of leadership. Americans deserve better. I therefore intend to oppose the effort to increase America's debt limit."

---

*Flop: As president, in April 2011, saying he regretted his previous position:* "Nobody likes to be tagged as having increased the debt limit for the United States by a trillion dollars. As president, you start realizing, you know what, we can't play around with this stuff. . . . [Raising the limit is] important for the country."

### Forty-Seven percent, which cost Mitt Romney the election:

*Leaked comments from a fund-raiser in May 2012:* "There are 47 percent of the people who will vote for the president no matter what. All right, there are 47 percent who are with him, who are dependent upon government, who believe that they are victims, who believe the government has a responsibility to care for them, who believe that they are entitled to health care, to food, to housing, to you-name-it. . . . My job is not to worry about those people. I'll never convince them they should take personal responsibility and care for their lives."

### Ron Johnson, defending Citizens United:

"If you want to be heard, sure you can set up a soapbox on the corner of a park and you can be heard. But it's a pretty limited audience. If you want your message to be heard by a wider group of Americans it costs money to broadcast that message." *(Devil's Advocates Radio Network, June 5, 2014)*

### Pete Stark, on power:

*At a town hall meeting in his district in California, July 24, 2010:* "The federal government, yes, can do most anything in this country." *(No surprise that his comment elicited a lot of boos.)*

### Rep. Fred Heineman (R-NC), explaining that his yearly income of $180,000 leaves him short of middle-class status:

"When I see a first-class individual who makes $80,000 a year, he's lower middle class. When I see someone who is making anywhere from $300,000 to $750,000 a year, that's middle class. When I see anyone above that, that's upper middle class." *(during the 1996 election)*

### Joe Barton (R-TX), addressing the CEO of BP after the 2010 oil spill, during congressional hearings:

"I think it is a tragedy of the first proportion that a private corporation can be subjected to what I would call a shakedown, in this case, a $20 billion dollar shakedown. I apologize." *(He apologized again that afternoon—for his comments above after Republican leadership threatened him with losing his committee status.)*

**Terri Lynn Land, former Republican candidate for Michigan State Senator, on Ford:**

I'm with [Romney] on that. Because, actually Bill Ford—we live with the autos. Michigan is a very unique state. No state has one industry that's so prominent and that's global. It's not a Michigan industry, it's global. And what basically happened is Bill Ford went and got a loan. I mean, he did it that way. And so people know that that could have been done. GM has become, they call it General Government basically, it's become this huge operation with really nobody that has the commitment like Bill Ford has with his family and his legacy of making sure that company is successful. And that's what it's kind of become. They call it Government Motors. That's what they call it.

---

That's the reality of it. I think that was the position to have and, you know, Ford is doing great. *(at the RNC in 2012)*

WHY CAN'T I JUST EAT MY WAFFLE?

# Chapter 6

## Sh*t Politicians Say About the Environment and Climate Change

"Trees cause more pollution than automobiles do."

—Ronald Reagan, 1981

While I'm not the granola-crunching type, I do love our planet. Unless we colonize Mars, or find Planet Earth 2, it's the only home we're going to have. And what I'm seeing is politicians denying the truth about climate change, which is destroying our only habitable planet and making lives miserable for millions of people around the world. Listening to stupid politicians talk, I think the groundwork was laid for not getting away from grimy oil and pollution a long while back.

### In Reagan's defense, there was no Google back then:

*Ronald Reagan,* Spokesman Review, *October 9, 1980, talking about pollution:* "I have flown twice over Mt. St. Helens out on our west coast. I'm not a scientist and I don't know the figures, but I have a suspicion that that one little mountain has probably released more sulfur dioxide into the atmosphere of the world than has been released in the last ten years of automobile driving or things of that kind that people are so concerned about." *(Note: Mount St. Helens, at its peak activity, emitted about 2,000 tons of sulfur dioxide per day, compared with 81,000 tons per day by cars.)*

### Lindsey Graham, on the Church of Climate-Changeology:

I believe climate change is real, but I reject the cap and trade solution of John . . . of, you know, of Al Gore. He's made a religion. It's a problem." (Fox News Sunday, *April 9, 2015*)

### Congresswoman Helen Chenoweth (R-ID), on job-blocking trees, during her 1994 campaign:

"Don't let anything like trees in the Clearwater National Forest get in the way of providing jobs and fueling the economy, even if that means cutting down every last tree in the state."

### Rep. Joe Barton (R-TX), rain ≠ climate:

*At an April 10, 2013, hearing discussing the Keystone XL pipeline:* "The Great Flood is an example of climate change. And that certainly wasn't because mankind overdeveloped hydrocarbon energy."

### Rep. Michele Bachmann, on carbon emissions, on the house floor in Washington, DC, on Earth Day:

"Carbon dioxide is portrayed as harmful. But there isn't even one study that can be produced that shows that carbon dioxide is a harmful gas." *(April 24, 2009)*

### Rep. John Shimkus (R-IL), um . . no:

*Uttered at a House subcommittee meeting on energy and environment, March 2009:* "So if we decrease the use of carbon dioxide, are we not taking away plant food from the atmosphere?"

Sh*t Politicians Say

### Rep. Joe Barton (R-TX), on wind:

"Wind is God's way of balancing heat. Wind is the way you shift heat from areas where it's hotter to areas where it's cooler. That's what wind is. Wouldn't it be ironic if in the interest of global warming we mandated massive switches to energy, which is a finite resource, which slows the winds down, which causes the temperature to go up? I mean, it does make some sense. You stop something, you can't transfer that heat, and the heat goes up. It's just something to think about." *(March 2009 congressional committee meeting)*

### On the BP oil spill in the Gulf of Mexico:

*Texas Governor Rick Perry, 2010:* "From time to time there are going to be things that occur that are acts of God that cannot be prevented."

---

*Pete Olson (R-TX), June 2010, on the moratorium on the BP oil spill:* "This is a kneejerk reaction by the administration to address a problem that doesn't exist."

### Louis Gohmert, on Caribou mating habits:

*When asked at the House National Resources Committee how a pipeline could affect local wildlife, February 2012, he replied:* "So when [caribou] want to go on a date, they invite each other to head over to the pipeline. . . . So my real concern now [is] if oil stops running through the pipeline . . . do we need a study to see how adversely the caribou would be affected if that warm oil ever quit flowing?"

### Bobby Jindal, on science denial, whatever that is:

The reality is, right now, we've got an administration—the Obama administration—that are science deniers when it comes to harnessing America's energy resources and the potential to create good-paying jobs. *(September 16, 2014, at a breakfast sponsored by the* Christian Science Monitor*)*

### Donald Trump on global warming (while I have nothing against my friend Don, he would agree he sometimes says stupid things):

"The very existence of global warming is BULLSHIT and needs to stop. Our planet is freezing, record low temps, and our GW scientists are stuck in ice." *(Twitter, January 1, 2014)*

———

"It's freezing and snowing in New York. We need global warming!" *(Twitter, November 7, 2012)*

———

"The concept of global warming was created by and for the Chinese in order to make US manufacturing non-competitive. *(Twitter, October 6, 2012)*

### Canadian Premier Rachel Notley of Alberta, on insulting your constituency:

*In a* Global News *interview, September 2015:* "We maintain the prosperity of our economy, but also make progress on our environment record. Like, real progress, so we can be genuinely proud that we are a leader as opposed to that embarrassing cousin no one wants to talk about." *(She later apologized.)*

### Rick Perry, on solar energy, and countries?:

"No greater example of it than this administration sending millions of dollars into the solar industry, and we lost that money. I want to say it was over $500 million that went to the country Solyndra." *(Iowa, December 12, 2011. BTW Solyndra is a solar panel company; he also mispronounced it!)*

### Sen. Ted Stevens (R-AK), on geographic area:

*Speaking about Hurricane Katrina, September 6, 2005:* "This is the largest disaster in the history of the United States, over an area twice the size of Europe. People have to understand this is a big, big problem." *(Note: neither New Orleans nor the Gulf States make up an area twice the size of Europe.)*

### Joe Barton, on what's causing man-made climate change:

"I don't deny that the climate is changing. I think you can have an honest difference of opinion on what's causing that change without automatically being either all-in that it's all because of mankind or it's all just natural. I think there's a divergence of evidence." *(speaking to the House Subcommittee on Energy and Power, April 10, 2013)*

### Ted Cruz, who needs to learn that weather and climate are two different things:

"You always have to be worried about something that is considered a so-called scientific theory that fits every scenario. Climate change, as they have defined it, can never be disproved, because whether it gets hotter or whether it gets colder, whatever happens, they'll say, well, it's changing, so it proves our theory." *(CNN, February 20, 2014)*

### Carly Fiorina, after the United States and China reached a deal to work together and lower carbon emissions:

"I think we have to read all the fine print. So every one of the scientists that tell us that climate change is real and being caused by manmade activity also tell us that a single nation, acting alone, can make no difference at all." *(August 21, 2015, in an interview with Katie Couric)*

**Rick Perry, even though 97 percent of scientists agree that climate change is real and manmade:**

"I do agree that the science is not settled on this. The idea that we would put Americans' economy at jeopardy based on scientific theory that's not settled yet, to me is just nonsense. Just because you have a group of scientists that stood up and said, this is the fact. Galileo got outvoted for a spell. But the fact is, to put America's economic future in jeopardy, asking us to cut back in areas that would have monstrous economic impact on this country, is not good economics, and I will suggest to you is not necessarily good science." *(September 8, 2012, GOP debate)*

**Rep. Joe Barton, questioning a Nobel Prize Laureate:**

*At a congressional hearing on climate change, Washington DC, April 23, 2009:* "I have one simple question and it will only take about six seconds to ask. How did all the oil and gas get to Alaska and under the Arctic Ocean." *(Nobel laureate Steven Chu responds that plate tectonics and geology over millions of years created oil and gas.* "Isn't it obvious that it was a lot warmer at one time in Alaska? I mean, it wasn't a big pipeline that we created in Texas and shipped up there, and then put it underground so we can now pump it out and ship it? . . . So it just drifted up there?"*)*

**Paul Broun (R-GA) thinks this line never gets old:**

"Scientists from all over the world say that the idea of human-induced global climate change is . . . a hoax." *(March 28, 2011)*

**Paul Broun, on science education:**

*Speaking at Liberty Baptist Church in Hartwell, Georgia, September 27, 2012:* "All that stuff I was taught about evolution, embryology, Big Bang Theory, all that is lies straight from the pit of Hell."

### On snowy winters:

*Ted Cruz, speaking to Seth Meyers on NBC, March 17, 2015:* "I just came back from New Hampshire where there's snow and ice everywhere. And my view actually is simple. Debates on this should follow science and should follow data. And many of the alarmists on global warming, they've got a problem because the science doesn't back them up. And in particular, satellite data demonstrate for the last 17 years there's been zero warming, none whatsoever."

---

*Steve King (R-IA) speaking at CPAC, during a snowless Winter Olympics in Vancouver!:* "The liberals, the environmentalists, the Al Gores of the world, were all wrong on science, and today we know it. . . . Sorry, Al. But I got a scoop shovel for you if you want to come to any of the fifty states in America. For the first time in the history of keeping records, there is snowfall on the ground in all fifty states. It is tough to make an argument when the evidence is all around us, the snowy white wonder in a crystal cathedral." *(February 19, 2010)*

### Ted Cruz remembers "global cooling" (or, scientific theories do not work that way):

"The last 15 years, there has been no recorded warming. Contrary to all the theories that they are expounding, there should have been warming over the last 15 years. It hasn't happened . . . You know, back in the '70s . . . I remember the '70s, we were told there was global cooling. And everyone was told global cooling was a really big problem. And then that faded. . . . You always have to be worried about something that is considered a so-called scientific theory that fits every scenario. Climate change, as they have defined it, can never be disproved, because whether it gets hotter or whether it gets colder, whatever happens, they'll say, well, it's changing, so it proves our theory." *(April 20, 2014, in an interview with CNN)*

### Mitt Romney, going from right to wrong:

*His view about global warming during a campaign stop in New Hampshire, June 2011:* "I don't speak for the scientific community, of course, but I believe the world's getting warmer. I can't prove that, but I believe based on what I read that the world is getting warmer. And number two, I believe that humans contribute to that. I don't know how much our contribution is to that, because I know that there have been periods of greater heat and warmth in the past but I believe we contribute to that. And so I think it's important for us to reduce our emissions of pollutants and greenhouse gases that may well be significant contributors to the climate change and the global warming that you're seeing."

––––––––––

*His views on global warming during a campaign stop in Pittsburgh, October 28, 2011:* "My view is that we don't know what's causing climate change on this planet. And the idea of spending trillions and trillions of dollars to try to reduce $CO_2$ emissions is not the right course for us."

### On environmental platforms:

*Lindsey Graham (R-SC), speaking to the Council on Foreign Relations, March 23, 2015:* "What is the environmental platform of the Republican Party? I don't know either."

### On carbon emissions:

*Washington State Republican Representative Ed Orcutt, proposing a tax on cyclists because he says it's less environmentally friendly than driving!:* "You would be giving off more $CO_2$ if you are riding a bike than driving a car." *(March 2, 2013)*

## Carly Fiorina, in an interview with Katie Couric, May 2015, on old-fashioned technology that's being phased out anyway:

"So we have to focus on how to make coal cleaner. Look, coal provides half the energy in this nation, still, not to mention around the world. So to say we're going to basically outlaw coal, which is what this administration has done, is so self-defeating. It destroys jobs, it destroys communities, it's not helping us, and it's not helping global warming. So let's get on with the innovation about how to make sure that we actually have clean coal technology."

## Ronald Reagan (then governor of California), on the Redwood Forest:

"A tree's a tree. How many more do you need to look at?" *(quoted in the* Sacramento Bee, *opposing expansion of Redwood National Park, March 3, 1966)*

---

*Then in September 1966:* "I don't believe a tree is a tree and if you've seen one you've seen them all."

## Marco Rubio, apparently not knowing Hillary's position:

*At a campaign stop in Salem, Ohio, October 16, 2015:* "This is what I mean when I say Democrats like Hillary Clinton are outdated. They label themselves 'progressives' yet take pride in opposing economic progress. Even their own constituencies are starting to wonder what's going on. When ballot measures have come up in Ohio to ban hydraulic fracturing, traditionally democratic groups such as labor unions have led the charge to defeat them." *(I guess he didn't get the memo that Hillary supports hydraulic fracking (even though many Dems wish she didn't.)*

# Chapter 7

## Sh*t Politicians Say About Foreign Affairs

"Congress is a very special group of people. More than 80 percent of them never left the United States."

—Sergey Lavrov, Russian Foreign Minister,
December 16, 2014, in an interview with
the French television network France 24

And that, above, in sum, is how the rest of the world sees us. If you want to know why, just read some of the quotes below. On both sides of the aisle, people mess up stupid little things that make America look dumb and ignorant.

### On keeping up with current events:

*Mike Huckabee, explaining why he was unfamiliar with the National Intelligence Estimate on Iran's nuclear capability:* "The point I'm trying to make is that, on the campaign trail, nobody's going to be able, if they've been campaigning as hard as we have been, to keep up with every single thing, from what happened to Britney last night to who won *Dancing with the Stars.*" *(Quad City Times, December 31, 2007)*

### On the British Embassy:

*Barack Obama, during a White House press briefing after an attack on the British Embassy, November 29, 2011:* "I think it's important for me to just note that all of us are deeply disturbed by the, uh, the, uh, crashing of the English Embassy, the Embassy of the United Kingdom in Iran." *(There is no "English Embassy.")*

### Dr. Ben Carson, on one-horse Russia:

"Putin is a one-horse, uh, country. Oil and energy." *(GOP debate, January 28, 2016)*

### Donald Trump, on China:

*During his presidential announcement, New York City, June 16, 2015:* "Our country is in serious trouble. We don't have victories anymore. We used to have victories, but we don't have them. When was the last time anybody saw us beating, let's say China in a trade deal? I beat China all the time. All the time."

———

*In response to his statement above about China:* "People say, 'You don't like China.' No, I love them. I just sold an apartment for $15 million to someone from China. Am I supposed to dislike them?"

### How many sides does an island have?

Joe Barton, not realizing Cuba has more than 1 shore: "Chinese oil companies are drilling off the coast of Cuba, which means they are drilling off the coast of Florida." *(June 15, 2010)*

### Being a hospitable former secretary of state:

*Madeline Albright in Prague, during a brush with activists:* "Disgusting Serbs. Get out!" *(October 23, 2012)*

### Mitt Romney, on Vietnam (or not):

"It was not my desire to go off and serve in Vietnam." *(as quoted in the* Boston Herald *in 1994; he received a deferment to work as a Mormon missionary in France instead of seeing combat.)*

---

"I longed in many respects to actually be in Vietnam and representing our country there." *(Reflecting in a 2007* Boston Globe *interview about what he was doing during the Vietnam War)*

### On Africa (WHICH IS NOT A COUNTRY FOR THE BILLIONTH TIME!):

*Joe Biden at the US-Africa Business Forum, August 5, 2014:* "There's no reason the nation of Africa cannot and should not join the ranks of the world's most prosperous nations in the near term, in the decades ahead. There is simply no reason."

### John McCain, on a border that doesn't exist:

"We have a lot of work to do. It's a very hard struggle, particularly given the situation on the Iraq-Pakistan border." *(The countries share no border and are practically on opposite sides of the Middle East. July 21, 2008)*

### John Kerry, on going to Iraq:

*Speaking to reporters at the Grand Canyon, August 9, 2004:* "Yes, I would have voted for the authority. I believe it was the right authority for a president to have. . . . [Although] I would have done this very differently from the way President Bush has."

---

*On ABC's* Good Morning America, *six weeks later:* "We should not have gone to war knowing the information that we know today. Knowing there was no imminent threat to America, knowing there were no weapons of mass destruction, knowing there was no connection of Saddam Hussein to al Qaeda, I would not have gone to war. That's plain and simple."

### Hillary Clinton, on voting to go to war in Iraq:

*Remarks during voting on the Senate floor, October 10, 2002:* "So it is with conviction that I support this resolution, as being in the best interest of our nation. A vote for it is not a vote to rush to war, it is a vote that puts awesome responsibility in the hands of our president. And we say to him: use these powers wisely and as a last resort."

———

*Senate floor speech on the war in Iraq, February 2, 2007:* "Four years ago, our president rushed us into war in Iraq. If I had been president in October of 2002, I would have never asked for authority to divert our attention from Afghanistan to Iraq and I certainly would never have started this war."

### Hillary Clinton, on Russians in Syria:

*On* Face the Nation, *September 20, 2015:* "I hope we're not turning to the Russians."

———

*Speaking in Iowa, October 6, 2015:* "I do believe and I've said this, that we should be putting together a coalition to support a no-fly zone. Because I, and look, I think it's complicated, and the Russians would have to be a part of it or it wouldn't work."

### Louis Gohmert (R-TX), on protecting endangered species:

*After Obama raised over $100 million for endangered animals, Gohmert said this on the House floor, April 2009:* "There is no assurance that if we did that we wouldn't end up with moo goo dog pan or moo goo cat pan. There is no way to assure that money will not be wasted when it's sent to foreign countries."

### Michele Bachmann, on a nation that doesn't exist anymore:

*On right-wing Christian attorney Jay Sekulow's radio show, 2011:* "What people recognize is that there's a fear that the United States is in an unstoppable decline. They see the rise of China, the rise of India, the rise of the Soviet Union and our loss militarily going forward." *(The Soviet Union collapsed in 1991.)*

### President Obama, on European politics and terminology:

*Answering a question from an Austrian reporter in Strasbourg, France, April 2009:* "It was also interesting to see that political interaction in Europe is not that different from the United States Senate. There's a lot of—I don't know what the term is in Austrian—wheeling and dealing." *(Austrian is not a real language, as Austrians speak German.)*

### Sarah Palin, on Glenn Beck's radio show, confused about which side we're on:

"But obviously, we've got to stand with our North Korean allies." *(Apparently confusing North and South Korea, November 24, 2010)*

### Rep. Hank Johnson (D-GA), expressing concern during a congressional hearing that the presence of a large number of American soldiers might disturb the island of Guam:

"My fear is that the whole island will become so overly populated that it will tip over and capsize." *(April 1, 2010)*

### President Ronald Reagan, on what he learned during a trip to Latin America:

"Well, I learned a lot. . . . I went down to [Latin America] to find out from them and [learn] their views. You'd be surprised.

They're all individual countries." *(question-and-answer session with reporters, December 4, 1982)*

### Rick Perry, on Juarez City:

*In a sit-down with reporters on February 28, 2011, Perry, governor of Texas, exclaimed:* "Juarez is reported to be the most dangerous city in America." *(Juarez is in Mexico.)*

### Louis Gohmert, on Mexican Terrorists:

*In an interview on C-SPAN's* Washington Journal *on April 17, 2013:* "We know Al Qaeda has camps with the drug cartels on the Mexican border . . . we know that people are now being trained to come in and act like Hispanic, when they are radical Islamists." *(There is no evidence this is happening.)*

### Rand Paul, on Middle Eastern Politics:

*In a statement on Fox News, February 11, 2015:* "I really do blame Hillary Clinton's war in Libya for creating a lot of the chaos that is now spreading throughout the Middle East." *(Have you heard any news about the Iraq Civil War? The coups and religious revolutions that have been taking place for the last forty to fifty years or more?)*

### Canadian politician Jim Prentice, on math:

*Addressing NDP's Rachel Notley (for non-Canadian readers, NDP is the National Democratic Party) in a debate about taxes, he quipped:* "I know that math is difficult." *(April 23, 2015)*

### Sheila Jackson Lee, on Vietnam:

*In a special order speech on the House floor, July 15, 2010:* "Today, we have two Vietnams, side by side, North and South, exchanging and working. We may not agree with all that North Vietnam is doing, but they are living in peace. I would look for a better human rights record for North Vietnam, but they are living side by side." *(This said over thirty years after Vietnam became one country under communist rule.)*

**Michele Bachmann, on African countries (See "Africa" above. I put it on another page just to highlight how annoying it is to hear it over and over from people who should know better):**

"The president, he put us in Libya. He is now putting us in Africa. We already were stretched too thin, and he put our special operations forces in Africa." *(CNN debate, October 2011)*

**Michele Bachmann, on pitfalls of the global economy (note, while I think the world is moving in this direction, I don't think Obama is the one behind it—or the only one):**

"Well, President Obama is trying to bind the United States into a global economy where all of our nations come together in a global economy. I don't want the United States to be in a global economy where, where our economic future is bound to that of Zimbabwe. I can't, we can't necessarily trust the decisions that are being made financially in other countries. . . . So I think clearly this is a very bad direction because when you join the economic policy of different nations, it is one short step to joining political unity and then you would have literally, a one world government, . . . I don't want to cede United States authority to a transnational organization." *(interview on Scott Hennen's radio show, June 29, 2010)*

# Chapter 8

# Sh*t Politicians Say About Same-Sex Rights and Gay Marriage

It's not any politician's business what goes on in other people's bedrooms. Alas, these politicians seem to think that they can play Peeping Tom and voyeur into Americans' sex lives. And if straight people can get married, why would we as a free country deny that right to lesbian and gay couples? It's stupid, stupid that was thankfully overturned last June, but the stupid stink still remains, unfortunately.

### Sen. Saxby Chambliss (R-GA), on marriage equality:

*When asked by reporters if his views on same-sex marriage have changed:* "I'm not gay, so I'm not going to marry one." *(March 2013)*

### Rick Santorum, on love and marriage:

"Is anyone saying same-sex couples can't love each other? I love my children. I love my friends, my brother. Heck, I even love my mother-in-law. Should we call these relationships marriage, too?" *(In a* Philadelphia Inquirer *column, May 2008)*

### Sen. Tim Scott (R-SC), what?:

*Arguing against the Affordable Care Act (ACA) at a local meeting, July 2012:* "We are faced with a president who believes that men and women, no matter their effort, should all be equal. You see, some of us believe in freedom. Others want equality." *(I still don't know what the ACA has to do with same-sex marriage.)*

### Louis Gohmert, speaking to Liberty University students and missing the point:

"Congress is good about having studies. How about if we take four heterosexual couples, and put them on an island where they have everything they need to live and exist, and we take four couples of just men and put them on an island where they have all they need to survive. And then let's take four couples of just women and put them on an island, and then let's come back in 100 years and see which one nature favors. Just see, you know?" *(November 2015)*

### Tony Perkins, head of the Family Research Council (FRC) (labeled a hate group by the Southern Poverty Law Center) on "It Gets Better":

"The videos are titled 'It Gets Better.' They are aimed at persuading kids that although they'll face struggles and perhaps bullying for 'coming out' as homosexual (or transgendered or some other perversion), life will get better. . . . It's disgusting. And it's part of a concerted effort to persuade kids that homosexuality is okay and actually to recruit them into that lifestyle." *(FRC fund-raising letter, August 2011)*

### Sen. Jesse Helms (R-NC), on Americans who contract AIDS:

*Why he opposed approval of the Ryan White CARE act, which funds AIDS research:* "We've got to have some common sense about a disease transmitted by people deliberately engaging in unnatural acts." *(July 5, 1995)*

### Jody Hice, on believing satire to be true:

*From his book,* It's Now or Never: A Call to Reclaim America, *2012:* "These shocking words by Michael Swift have been considered part of the 'gay manifesto' by many, and reveal the radical agenda that is currently threatening our nation. . . . One need not look very far to discover the overall agenda of militant homosexuality, and its attempt to permanently change American society." *(Note: Hice was commenting on a satirical piece by a gay writer that poked fun at the idea of a gay agenda. However, he neglected to mention that Swift's piece was satire. I guess he didn't get the joke.)*

### Louis Gohmert, on "Don't Ask, Don't Tell" repeal:

*On the Christian talk-radio show* Point of View *on October 21, 2014, Congressman Gohmert went on a homophobic rant:* "Hey, you know, there's nothing wrong with gays in the military. Look at the Greeks. Well, you know, they did have people come along who they loved that was the same sex and would give them massages before they went into battle. But you know what, it's a different kind of fighting, it's a different kind of war and if you're sitting around getting massages all day ready to go into a big, planned battle, then you're not going to last very long. It's guerrilla fighting. You are going to be ultimately vulnerable to terrorism and if that's what you start doing in the military like the Greeks did . . . as people have said, 'Louie, you have got to understand, you don't even know your history.' Oh yes I do. I know exactly. It's not a good idea." *(October 21, 2014)*

### Charles Van Zant (R-FL), on the hidden agenda of the Common Core:

*Speaking to crowds at the Operation Education Rescue conference in Orlando, Florida, March 22, 2014:* "These people will promote double-mindedness in state education and attract every one of your children to become as homosexual as they possibly can."

### Obama on same-sex marriage, varying opinions:

*For it:* "I favor legalizing same-sex marriages, and will fight efforts to prohibit such marriages." *(In answer to a questionnaire in* Chicago's Outlines. *At the time he was running for state senator in 1996.)*

---

*Against it: At the Saddleback Presidential Forum during his first run for president, Obama said:* "I believe marriage is between a man and a woman. Now, for me, as a Christian, it is also a sacred union." *(But he said he would support civil unions, April 17, 2008.)*

---

*For it again:* "I've just concluded that for me personally it is important for me to go ahead and affirm that I think same-sex couples should be able to get married." *(in an interview with Robin Roberts of* Good Morning America, *May 9, 2012)*

### Marco Rubio, on discrimination:

*Flip:* "The flip side is, should a photographer be punished for refusing to do a wedding that their faith teaches them is not one that is valid in the eyes of God? Here you're talking about the definition of an institution, not the value of a single human being. That's the difference between the civil rights movement and the marriage equality movement." *(appearing on Fox News's* The Five, *in March 2015)*

---

*Flop:* "I don`t believe that gay Americans should be denied services at a restaurant or hotel or anything of that nature. I also don't believe, however, that a caterer or photographer should be punished by the state for refusing to provide services for a gay

Sh*t Politicians Say

wedding because of their religious beliefs. We've got to figure out a way to protect that, as well." *(March 2015* Fox & Friends*)*

### Good ol' Mike Huckabee checking in:

"There's never been a civilization that has rewritten what marriage and family means and survived." (GQ *magazine, December 2, 2007)*

---

*Putting homosexuals in the same boat as necrophiliacs in his 1998 book* Kids Who Kill*:* "It is now difficult to keep track of the vast array of publicly endorsed and institutionally supported aberrations—from homosexuality and pedophilia to sadomasochism and necrophilia."

### Sen. Rick Santorum (R-PA), arguing in favor of congressional efforts to pass a constitutional amendment banning marriage equality:

"Isn't that the ultimate homeland security, standing up and defending marriage?" *(July 2004)*

### Carl Paladino, New York State Tea Party-backed candidate for governor, rehashing the "Think of the Children" cliché:

*At a campaign rally in Williamsburg, New York, while running for governor (in a really liberal state):* "I just think my children, and your children, will be much better off, and much more successful getting married and raising a family. And I don't want them to be brainwashed into thinking that homosexuality is an equally valid or successful option. It isn't." *(October 10, 2010)*

### Rand Paul, on more businesses discriminating:

*Taking issue with the Civil Rights Act of 1964 while arguing that government should not prevent private businesses from discriminating on the basis of race:* "I don't want to be associated with those people, but I also don't want to limit their speech in any way in the sense that we tolerate boorish and uncivilized behavior because that's one of the things freedom requires is that we allow people to be boorish and uncivilized, but that doesn't mean we approve of it." *(interview with MSNBC's Rachel Maddow, May 21, 2010)*

### Rick Santorum, comparing gay marriage to 9/11:

"[Gay marriage] is an issue just like 9/11. . . . We didn't decide we wanted to fight the war on terrorism because we wanted to. It was brought to us. And if not now, when? When the supreme courts in all the other states have succumbed to the Massachusetts version of the law?" *(interview with the* Allentown Morning Call, *February 2004)*

### Rep. Steve King, about gun magazine limits having something to do with LGBT rights:

*In a conference call with Rick Scarborough, founder of Tea Party Unity, discussing a proposed gun magazine limit (or at least, it starts out that way):* "And I pointed out, well, once you make it ten, then why would you draw the line at ten? What's wrong with nine? Or eleven? And the problem is once you draw that limit—it's kind of like marriage when you say it's not a man and a woman anymore, then why not have three men and one woman, or four women and one man, or why not somebody has a love for an animal? There is no clear place to draw the line once you eliminate the traditional marriage, and it's the same once you start putting limits on what guns can be used, then it's just really easy to have laws that make them all illegal." *(April 2, 2013)*

### Donald Trump, on marriage equality:

*Telling the* New York Times *why he opposes marriage equality:* "It's like in golf. A lot of people—I don't want this to sound trivial—but a lot of people are switching to these really long putters, very unattractive. It's weird. You see these great players with these really long putters, because they can't sink three-footers anymore. And, I hate it. I am a traditionalist. I have so many fabulous friends who happen to be gay, but I am a traditionalist." *(May 2, 2011)*

### The evolution of Hillary Clinton on marriage equality:

*During the Democratic presidential debate, October 2015, moderator Anderson Cooper, asked Clinton about her flip-flops, wondering if she would say anything to get votes. She responded:* "Well, actually, I have been very consistent . . . to the same values and principles. . . . But like most human beings—including those of us who run for office—I do absorb new information. I do look at what's happening in the world." *(So without further ado . . .)*

---

*At a news conference in White Plains, New York, January 2000:* "Marriage has got historic, religious, and moral content that goes back to the beginning of time and I think a marriage is as a marriage has always been, between a man and a woman."

---

*During a 2004 Senate floor debate about a proposed amendment to ban marriage equality (she opposed the amendment, but still defined marriage as between a man and a woman):* "I take umbrage at anyone who might suggest that those of us who worry about amending the Constitution are less committed to the sanctity of marriage, or the fundamental bedrock principle that [marriage] exists between a man and a woman, going back into the midst of history as one of the founding, foundational institutions of history and humanity and civilization, and that its primary, principal role during those millennia has been the raising and socializing of children for the society into which they are to become adults."

---

*Filming a Human Rights Campaign (HRC) (an organization that supports rights for LGBT people) video supporting same-sex marriage, 2013:* "LGBT Americans are our colleagues, our teachers, our soldiers, our friends, our loved ones. And they are full and equal citizens, and they deserve the rights of citizenship. That includes marriage. That's why I support marriage for lesbian and gay couples. I support it personally and as a matter of policy and law, embedded in a broader effort to advance equality and opportunity for LGBT Americans and all Americans."

---

*And in a 2014 interview with NPR:* "Marriage had always been a matter left to the states. And in many of the conversations that I and my colleagues and supporters had, I fully endorse the efforts by activists who work state-by-state."

### Mitt Romney, introducing the far-right pundit Ann Coulter at the Conservative Political Action Conference on March 2, 2007:

"I'm happy to learn that after I speak you're going to hear from Ann Coulter. That's a good thing. I think it's important to get the views of moderates." *(. . . right before Coulter called John Edwards a "f\*ggot")*

### Tony Perkins (him again), on repealing "Don't Ask, Don't Tell":

*May 2010, speaking with John McCain about his opposition to allowing LGBT individuals to openly serve in the military:* "Absolutely, without question—I know a lot of people point to militaries that have allowed homosexuality within the ranks—there's twenty-five of almost two hundred nations, but the top militaries in the world do not allow homosexuality to be openly engaged in, in the military—I mean, if you want a military that just does parades and stuff like that then I guess that's okay."

### Condescending jerks:

*After being asked by the president of Waverly High School Gay-Straight Alliance why she wouldn't support marriage equality, Michele Bachmann replied:* "They can get married. They can marry a man if they're a woman. Or they can marry a woman if they're a man." *(November 30, 2011)*

---

*Responding to a question about the AIDS crisis posed by the AP while running for Senate, Mike Huckabee said in 1992:* "It is difficult to understand the public policy towards AIDS. It is the first time in the history of civilization in which the carriers of a genuine plague have not been isolated from the general population, and in which this deadly disease for which there is no cure is being treated as a civil rights issue instead of the true health crisis it represents."

### Rick Perry believes being gay is a choice:

"There is a land of opportunity, friends—it's called Texas. We're creating more jobs than any other state in the nation. Would you rather live in a state like this, or a state where guys can marry guys?" *(on the campaign trail, August 30, 2010)*

---

*In his 2008 book,* On My Honor, *comparing homosexuality to alcoholism:* "Even if an alcoholic is powerless over alcohol once it enters his body, he still makes a choice to drink. And, even if someone is attracted to a person of the same sex, he or she still makes a choice to engage in sexual activity with someone of the same gender."

### Arnold Schwarzenegger, missing the point:

"I think gay marriage is something that should be between a man and a woman." *(interview with Sean Hannity, Fox News, 2002)*

## Tony Perkins (yet again) on musicals:

*In a statement about members of the UN seeing* Fun Home *the musical:* "It was a stunning display of political tone deafness, considering the real crises happening right now on the real world stage. Unfortunately, as far as this president is concerned, the most urgent message America can send to the international community right now is 'that protecting the rights of LGBT people will remain a key foreign policy priority of the United States.' And its only priority, seemingly. While the world is experiencing the largest forced migration since WWII, the White House can't bring itself to say much about the persecution endured by men and women of faith." *(March 4, 2016)*

## Homophobia masquerading as "persecution complex" greatest hits:

*Rep. Michele Bachmann, CPAC conference, March 2014:* "The thing that I think that is getting a little tiresome is, the gay community thinks that they've so bullied the American people and they so intimidated politicians that politicians fear them, and so they think that they get to dictate the agenda everywhere."

----

*Ted Cruz, in an interview with Christian Broadcast Network's David Brody, July 2013:* "If you look at other nations that have gone down the road towards gay marriage, that's the next step of where it gets enforced. It gets enforced against Christian pastors who decline to perform gay marriages, who speak out and preach biblical truths on marriage, that has been defined elsewhere as hate speech, as inconsistent with the enlightened view of government."

----

*Bobby Jindal, in response to the SCOTUS decision to strike down the Defense of Marriage Act (DOMA), June 28, 2015:* "I think it's offensive to equate evangelical Christians, Catholics, others that view marriage as between a man and a woman, as being racist, We're not racist. We love our fellow man, we think we're all equal under God's eyes, we don't believe we should change the definition of marriage simply because of opinion polls or because of a court that quite frankly isn't looking at the Constitution."

---

*Pat Buchanan, September 3, 1989, from "The New Morality and Barney Frank":* "Homosexuality involves sexual acts most men consider not only immoral, but filthy. The reason public men rarely say aloud what most say privately is they are fearful of being branded 'bigots' by an intolerant liberal orthodoxy that holds, against all evidence and experience, that homosexuality is a normal, healthy lifestyle."

---

*Pat Buchanan, October 17, 1990:* "With 80,000 dead of AIDS, our promiscuous homosexuals appear literally hell-bent on Satanism and suicide."

---

*Rick Santorum, quoted in the* Pittsburgh Post-Gazette, *July 2004:* "You can say I'm a hater. But I would argue I'm a lover. I'm a lover of traditional families and of the right of children to have a mother and father. . . . I would argue that the future of America hangs in the balance, because the future of the family hangs in the balance. Isn't that the ultimate homeland security, standing up and defending marriage?"

---

*Jody Hice, from his book,* It's Now or Never: A Call to Reclaim America, *2012:* "The concept of 'love' is not the issue when it comes to marriage! People love all kinds of other people and things, but that does not grant permission for marriage. It is illegal to marry a child or a sibling. It is illegal to marry a pet, which many people love dearly."

———————

*Mike Huckabee, CNN, February 1, 2015:* "When Christians are asked to accept gay marriage it's like asking someone who's Jewish to start serving bacon-wrapped shrimp in their deli. We don't want to do that—I mean, we're not going to do that. Or like asking a Muslim to serve up something that is offensive to him, or to have dogs in his backyard."

———————

*Marco Rubio, in a December 2015 interview with Chuck Todd on* Meet the Press: "It's not about discrimination. It is about the definition of a very specific, traditional, and age-old institution."

———————

*More from Jody Hice,* It's Now or Never: A Call to Reclaim America, *2012 (seems like a fun read!):* "Some ask the question, 'How does same-sex "marriage" threaten your marriage? . . . The answer is similar to asking, 'How does a trashy neighborhood affect you?' It might not affect you at all on a personal level. But, we are not talking about 'a' same-sex marriage. We are talking about an effort to redefine marriage, and that would have drastic results and irreversible consequences!"

———————

*And wrapping up this chapter with another one from Tony Perkins, in a January 2012 statement against BioWare's decision to allow gamers to play as homosexual characters:* "It makes no sense that BioWare and Electronic Arts would shatter that family quality in Star Wars video games just to . . . appease radical homosexual extremists."

THEY MISUNDERESTIMATED ME

# Chapter 9

## Sh*t Politicians Say About Health Care

While there's stuff in the Affordable Care Act (Or the ACA or Obamacare) that I'm not a fan of, that you're not a fan of, that no one's a fan of, it's given way to a lot of hyperbole and wacky conspiracy theories that just sound stupid. Worse—sound like fear mongering. To be fair, though, I've included some hyperbole and flat-out lies from the people who proposed or supported this bill (no provision for making people pay, my ass!).

### Freudian Slip from Rep. Paul Ryan:

*Announcing the 2014 proposed House budget plan on March 12, 2013, he uttered this slip-up:* "We're not going to give up on destroying the health-care system for the American people."

### On paying for health care:

*Sen. Sue Lowden (R-NV), on a local Nevada TV station, April 19, 2010, sharing her views on funding health care:* "Before we started having health care, in the olden days, when our grandparents would bring a chicken to the doctor. They would say, 'I'll paint your house.' Those were the old days of what people would do to get health care. And doctors are very sympathetic people, so I'm not backing down from that system."

### On Obamacare:

*Rand Paul, printed in a May 2, 2014, newsletter:* "Since the implementation of Obamacare, hundreds of thousands of Kentuckians have received cancellation notices from their current health care providers. For every Kentuckian that has enrolled in Obamacare, 40 have been dropped from their coverage. Obamacare has been presented to the American people through twisted rhetoric, smoke and mirrors. Obamacare is not good for America and it certainly [is] not good for Kentucky. I would like [to] hear how Obamacare affected you, your family or your small business." *(Via Politifact, May 5, 2014. Rand's claim is mathematically impossible.)*

### Ron Paul says beware the army of bureaucrats!:

"Just think about it, 16,500 armed bureaucrats coming to make [The Affordable Care Act] work" *(Fox News, March 2010)*

### Obamacare never asked me. I feel a little left out:

*Betsy McCaughey wrote in an op-ed called "Obamacare Will Question Your Sex Life" in the* New York Post: "Are you sexually active? If so, with one partner, multiple partners or same-sex partners? Be ready to answer those questions and more the next time you go to the doctor, whether it's the dermatologist or the cardiologist and no matter if the questions are unrelated to why you're seeking medical help. And you can thank the Obama health law." *(September 26, 2015)*

### Newt Gingrich, on hyperbole:

*Speaking against the Affordable Care Act, in March 2010 to whoever would listen:* "The most radical social experiment . . . in modern times. They will have destroyed their party much as Lyndon Johnson shattered the Democratic Party for 40 years with the enactment of civil rights legislation in the 1960s."

### Rand Paul, on SCOTUS's powers, June 28, 2012:

"Just because a couple people on the Supreme Court declare something to be 'constitutional' does not make it so. The whole thing remains unconstitutional. While the court may have erroneously come to the conclusion that the law is allowable, it certainly does nothing to make this mandate or government takeover of our health care right." *(Actually, that's sort of SCOTUS's job, to decide if something is constitutional or not. Did you not show up to Civics 101 on the day they covered this?)*

### Is Ted Cruz, trying to make his own collection of Bushisms?:

*Speaking at a Q&A Session at a Red State Convention, August 5, 2013:* "Buzzfeed—the left-wing site—y'all know Buzzfeed? Yesterday they did a whole series of graphic pictures basically showing that I was promised one thing on Obamacare and here is what I'm left with." *(Note: his comments concerned a post by the Heritage Foundation, a conservative think tank, that were posted on Buzzfeed.)*

### Michele Bachmann, on really tall doctors and the IRS:

*At an appearance in Webster City, Iowa, on November 16, 2011, Bachmann claimed:* "One man stood up, he was over seven feet tall. He was a physician in the community. And he said, 'I had a little lady in my office and because of Obamacare, I had to call the IRS and I had to get a number to put on a form before I could see her.'" *(Are you putting us on, Michele?)*

### Congressman John Dingell, on the people:

*In an interview on radio station WJR, March 23, 2010, Dingell let this doozie slip:* "The harsh fact of the matter is when you're passing legislation that will cover 300 million American people in different ways, it takes a long time to do the necessary administrative steps that have to be taken to put the legislation together to control the people."

### Ben Carson, on hyperbole:

"Obamacare is the worst thing that has happened in this nation since slavery. In a way, it is slavery, because it is making all of us subservient to the government." *(October 11, 2013, Values Voters Summit)*

### Rand Paul, on a similarly themed enslavement via health care:

*At a Senate Health, Education, and Labor Committee hearing, on May 11, 2011, he argued against the ACA because he thinks it will "enslave him." Here is his reasoning:* "With regard to the idea of whether you have a right to health care, you have [to] realize what that implies. It's not an abstraction. I'm a physician. That means you have a right to come to my house and conscript me. It means you believe in slavery. It means that you're going to enslave not only me, but the janitor at my hospital, the person who cleans my office, the assistants who work in my office, the nurses. . . . I'm a physician in your community and you say you have a right to health care. You have a right to beat down my door with the police, escort me away and force me to take care of you? That's ultimately what the right to free health care would be."

### Rep. Louis Gohmert (R-TX), on Socialism:

"We've been battling this socialist health care, this nationalization of health care, that is absolutely going to kill senior citizens. They'll put them on lists and force them to die early." *(from the* Alex Jones Show, *July 26, 2009)*

## On Romneycare:

*Mitt Romney while campaigning for president in Baltimore in 2007:* "I'm proud of what we've done. If Massachusetts succeeds in implementing [Romneycare], then that will be a model for the nation."

----

*Mitt Romney in a 2011 Republican presidential primary debate:* "At the time I crafted the plan in the last campaign I was asked is [Romneycare] something that you would have the whole nation do, and I said no. This is something that was crafted for Massachusetts. It would be wrong to adopt this as a nation."

## Mitt Romney, on supporting/opposing Obamacare (that was fast):

"Well, I'm not getting rid of all of health-care reform." *(Meet the Press interview, September 9, 2012)*

----

*Here he is, the next day:* "Obamacare must be repealed in its entirety." *(Hugh Hewitt Show interview, September 10, 2012)*

## Bill Cassidy (R-LA), on the uninsured:

*At the Louisiana Oil and Gas Association's annual meeting, March 20, 2014:* "The uninsured are relatively less sophisticated, less comfortable with forms, less educated."

## Joni Ernst (R-IA), on Medicaid/Medicare recipients (or, that's a lot of voters):

*In Des Moines, Iowa, arguing against Medicaid expansion in the state on April 2, 2014, she made a claim about a lot of her constituency:* "Iowa has nearly 500,000 Medicaid enrollees. If the program is expanded, it is estimated the Medicaid population will grow by an additional 110,000 to 181,000 recipients who have no personal responsibility for their health and no accountability for the care provided."

### Sen. Chuck Grassley (R-IA), on Obamacare death panels:

*At a town hall in Iowa on August 12, 2009, Grassley joined the "death panel" conspiracy theorists:* "We should not have a government program that determines if you're going to pull the plug on Grandma."

### Oklahoma Rep. Jim Bridenstine (R-OK), actually, it does:

*When asked in an interview with* The Daily Caller *in March 2013 about SCOTUS and the legal status of Obamacare:* "Just because the Supreme Court rules on something doesn't necessarily mean that that's constitutional." *(See Rand Paul's quote above. Another guy who must have slept in that college class.)*

### Congresswoman Debbie Wasserman Schultz, on the ACA:

*In a town hall meeting on April 5, 2010, addressing the newly passed ACA:* "We actually have not required in this law that you carry health insurance." *(Actually, having health insurance, as most of you reading this know, is a staple of the law. The rest of you, I can't help!)*

### Sen. Tom Colburn (R-OK), on the health benefits of fake boobs:

*In a Senate Judiciary Committee meeting to restrict lawsuits, February 1, 2005:* "I thought I would just share with you what science says today about silicone breast implants. If you have them, you're healthier than if you don't."

### Rand Paul, on writing legislation:

*Appearing on Fox News, August 13, 2013, talking about the Affordable Care Act:* "The way our country works is that legislation is written by Congress, passed by your representatives, the president doesn't get to write legislation, and it's illegal and unconstitutional for him to change legislation himself." *(According to the SCOTUS case* Heckler v. Chaney, *it IS constitutional for the president to delay enforcement/enactment of parts of laws.)*

**And finally, speaking of Cruz, let's enjoy highlights from his twenty-one-hour filibuster of the ACA (or, a study in sleep deprivation), on the US Senate floor, September 24, 2013:**

*On his attempts to defund Obamacare:* "Each day I learn what a scoundrel I am."

---

*Preparing to pull an all-nighter filibustering:* "I'll talk until I can't stand anymore. Don't worry, I have government-run health insurance. I'll be fine."

---

"I don't get to read it that often because I tell them, 'Go pick the books you want to read and I read it to them,' But since tonight, girls, you aren't here, you don't get to pick the book, so I get to pick *Green Eggs and Ham*."

---

"*Green Eggs and Ham* was my favorite book as a little boy. You can actually do it—the food coloring is a little bit cheating. But if you take spinach and mix it into the eggs, the eggs turn green."

---

"Our veterans should be above politics. It is shameful that the administration is barricading and trying to shut down the memorials."

"The moon might be as intimidating as Obamacare."

---

"Twenty years from now if there is some obscure Trivial Pursuit question, I am confident I will be the answer." *(If the question was: Who lost it for twenty-plus hours on the Senate floor?)*

---

"Millions of Americans tune into *Duck Dynasty* so I want to point out just a few words of wisdom from *Duck Dynasty*. . . . Jay said Redneck rule No. 1 . . . most things can be fixed with duct tape and extension cords. That's actually very true."

---

"I like their little burgers. . . . I'm a big fan of eating White Castle burgers. Think of all the people that don't get jobs because there's no White Castle open, not to mention all of the hungry college kids that at 3:00 in the morning are just craving a White Castle, and they can't find one." *(Probably said this at 3:00 in the morning.)*

---

"It's a little bit like the World Wrestling Federation. It's wrestling matches where . . . the outcome is prerigged, the outcome is predetermined. They know who's going to win and it's all for show."

---

"Some time ago I tweeted a speech that Ashton Kutcher gave. It's a terrific speech. It was a speech at one of these award shows where he talked about the value of hard work. And one of the things I remember he said is he said, you know, in my life, opportunity looks an awful lot like hard work. That was a great message. It was a great message to young people . . . I don't know Mr. Kutcher.

I've watched his TV shows and his movies. I don't know him personally, but you know what? He can speak to millions of young people who've never listened to you and would never listen to me."

———

"If you go to the 1940s, Nazi Germany. Look, we saw in Britain, Neville Chamberlain, who told the British people, 'Accept the Nazis. Yes, they'll dominate the continent of Europe but that's not our problem. Let's appease them. Why? Because it can't be done. We can't possibly stand against them.'"

———

"I don't know if it's the water, something in the air, the cherry blossoms, but people get here [Washington, DC] and they stop listening to the American people."

———

"I wondered if at some point we were going to see a tall gentleman in a mechanical breathing apparatus come forward and say in a deep voice say, 'Mike Lee, I am your father' . . . and just like in *Star Wars* movies the empire will strike back."

———

"You might think a camel's hairbrush must be made of camels. But a camel's hairbrush is made of squirrel fur, and it makes you wonder . . . the squirrels apparently have a very bad marketing department."
*(If I were a Senator on September 24, 2013, I bet I would have wished I called in sick that day!)*

# Chapter 10

# *Sh\*t Politicians Say About Civil Rights Issues*

I've heard a lot of crazy shit from politicians about taking civil rights away, from being racist to defending torture. I find it un-American and really, really stupid.

### On voter fraud:

*Sen. Benjamin Ryan Tillaman, admitting in February 1900 to election tampering to prevent African Americans from voting:* "We have done our level best. . . . We have scratched our heads to find out how we could eliminate the last one of them. We stuffed ballot boxes. We shot them. We are not ashamed of it."

### President Eisenhower, stereotyping:

*To Chief Justice Earl Warren at a White House dinner, 1954, commenting on racial segregation after the* Brown v. Board of Education *decision:* "These are not bad people. All they are concerned about is to see that their sweet little girls are not required to sit in school alongside some big overgrown Negroes."

### About waterboarding:

*Rick Santorum, in an interview on May 17, 2011, with Hugh Hewitt on his radio show:* "John McCain doesn't understand how enhanced interrogation works. I mean, you break somebody, and after they're broken, they become cooperative." *(John McCain*

121

*was a POW and endured torture. Santorum backtracked his criticism two days later, saying:* "For anyone to infer my disagreement with Senator McCain's policy position lessens my respect for his service to our country and all he had to endure is outrageous and unfortunate.")

---

*Peter King, in a radio show appearance, December 9, 2014, discussing a senate report on CIA torture:* "We're not talking about anyone being burned or stabbed or cut or anything like that. We're talking about people being made to stand in awkward positions, have water put into their nose and into their mouth. But again, nobody suffered any lasting injuries from this." *(Politifact rates this one "Pants on Fire.")*

## On invasion from Mexico:

*Pat Buchanan, from the book* Suicide of a Superpower, *2011:* "Mexico is moving north. Ethnically, linguistically, and culturally, the verdict of 1848 is being overturned. Will this Mexican nation within a nation advance the goals of the Constitution—to 'insure domestic tranquility' and 'make us a more perfect union'? Or has our passivity in the face of this invasion imperiled our union?"

## Louis Gohmert, on the invasion of Marxist teachers:

*In a radio interview with Joyce Kaufman, February 10, 2016:* "That's also because we let some of the hippies from the '60s who created such chaos then start teaching the teachers, and teaching them how great socialism is and just rewriting history and keeping them from realizing socialism has never worked, it will never work in this world, in this life, because if you're going to pay everybody the same thing then they're going to quit working."

### On the Muslim Brotherhood:

*Louis Gohmert, speaking on WND Radio, April 26, 2013:* "The Obama administration has so many Muslim Brotherhood members . . . they are just making the wrong decisions for America."

———

*Pat Buchanan, from* Suicide of a Superpower, *2011:* "Those who believe the rise to power of an Obama rainbow coalition of peoples of color means the whites who helped to engineer it will steer it are deluding themselves. The whites may discover what it is like to ride in the back of the bus."

———

*Jody Hice, from his book,* It's Now or Never: A Call to Reclaim America, *2012:* "Although terror is a real threat and must be taken seriously, the worst plan is the Muslim Brotherhood's attempt to take over America! Don't think that it can't happen. Europe once considered itself impervious to Islam. Today we are being told that Europe will be 20 percent Islamic by mid-century because they were ignorant to the problem until It was too late. The United States had better wake up to the fact that this threat is real!"

### Bobby Jindal, on letting businesses discriminate:

*In a speech at the Ronald Reagan Presidential Foundation and Library in California on February 13, 2014:* "Under the Obama regime, the president and his allies are intentional in pursuing these conflicts from the perspective that you must sacrifice your most sacred beliefs to government the instant you start a business. You have the protection of the First Amendment as an individual, you see—but the instant you start a business, you lose those protections."

### On voter IDs:

*Mike Huckabee, at a Libertarian gathering in New Hampshire on April 2014:* "My gosh, I'm beginning to think that there's more freedom in North Korea sometimes than there is in the United States. When I go to the airport, I have to get in the surrender position, people put hands all over me, and I have to provide photo ID and a couple of different forms and prove that I really am not going to terrorize the airplane—but if I want to go vote I don't need a thing."

### On Obama:

*White ex-Illinois Gov. Rod Blagojevich, in an interview with* Esquire *magazine, January 2010:* "I'm blacker than Barack Obama. I shined shoes. I grew up in a five-room apartment. My father had a little Laundromat in a black community not far from where we lived. I saw it all growing up."

### Donald Trump, on protesters:

*After kicking out an overweight protester at a rally:* "You know, it's amazing, I mention food stamps and that guy who's seriously over-weight went crazy. He went crazy. Amazing." *(November 23, 2015)*

### John McCain, on wiretapping:

*Against wiretapping:* "I think that presidents have the obligation to obey and enforce laws that are passed by Congress and signed into law by the president, no matter what the situation is. I don't think the president has the right to disobey any law." *(Boston Globe, December 20, 2007)*

---

Sh*t Politicians Say

*Six months later, defending Bush for legalizing wiretapping:* "Neither the administration nor the telecoms need apologize for actions that most people, except for the ACLU and the trial lawyers, understand were constitutional and appropriate in the wake of the attacks on September 11, 2001." *(New York Times, June 6, 2008)*

### Phil Gingrey, on ebola in an open letter to the Centers for Disease Control (CDC), July 7, 2014:

"As you know, the United States is currently experiencing a crisis at our southern border. The influx of families and unaccompanied children at the border poses many risks, including grave public health threats. . . . Reports of illegal migrants carrying deadly diseases such as swine flu, dengue fever, Ebola virus and tuberculosis are particularly concerning" *(Phil fails Geography. Ebola is native to West Africa, not Latin America.)*

### Mitt Romney, on poverty in America:

"I'm not concerned about the very poor. We have a safety net there." *(CNN interview, January 2012)*

### On racism:

*Ted Cruz, at the Fox News GOP debate, March 3, 2016:* "It's every bit as true now as it was then. We need 100 more like Jesse Helms in the US Senate." *(Helms was a pro-segregationist senator that filibustered Martin Luther King Day.)*

––––––––––

*Bobby Jindal at CPAC, 2013:* "People say both Obama and I have trouble laughing at ourselves. We can't laugh at ourselves. That would be racist!"

### Jody Hice, on Islamophobia:

*From his book,* It's Now or Never: A Call to Reclaim America, *2012:* Although Islam has a religious component, it is much more than a simple religious ideology. It's a complete geopolitical structure and, as such, does not deserve First Amendment protection." *From a 2011 Coweta County Tea Party Patriots event:* "Most people think Islam is a religion, it's not. It's a totalitarian way of life with a religious component."

### Steve King (R-IA), on third-world stereotypes:

*During a tele-townhall meeting July 24, 2012, when asked about his views on Obama's birth certificate:* "We went down into the Library of Congress and we found a microfiche there of two newspapers in Hawaii each of which had published the birth of Barack Obama. It would have been awfully hard to fraudulently file the birth notice of Barack Obama being born in Hawaii and get that into our public libraries and that microfiche they keep of all the newspapers published. That doesn't mean there aren't some other explanations on how they might've announced that by telegram from Kenya. The list goes on."

### On diversity:

*Bill Jarvis, ex-Wildrose candidate, Canada, during a photo shoot, April 2002:* "We need lots of brown people in the front." *(The comment got him removed from his party!)*

### Mike Huckabee, on Trayvon Martin:

*Posted to Facebook, July 17, 2013:* "Trayvon Martin is not a hero. He was a young man whose life ended way too soon maybe because he decided to confront a man he believed was showing him disrespect."

### On the death penalty:

*Mike Christian (R-OK)* in response to a *forty-three-minute botched execution in his state, April 2014:* "I really don't care if it's by lethal injection, by the electric chair, firing squad, hanging, the guillotine, or being fed to the lions."

### Mitt Romney, on gun control:

*In a 2002 gubernatorial debate:* "We do have tough gun laws in Massachusetts. I support them. I won't chip away at them."

———

*In a 2008 interview with conservative bloggers:* "I don't support any gun control legislation, the effort for a new assault weapons ban, with a ban on semiautomatic weapons, is something I would oppose."

### Supreme Court Justice Earl Warren, 1942, justifying the Japanese internment camps:

"I take the view that this lack (of enemy subversive activity in the west coast) is the most ominous sign in our whole situation. It convinces me more than perhaps any other factor that the sabotage we are to get, the Fifth Column activities are to get, are timed just like Pearl Harbor. . . . I believe we are just being lulled into a false sense of security."

### About building a wall along the Mexican border (apparently nothing new):

*Steve King, at a 2010 Tea Party rally:* "I told this to Karl Rove one day, we were having this discussion. I said, Karl, if you give me $6 million a mile, there will not be a cockroach [that will] get across my mile. I guarantee it!"

———

*Herman Cain, campaign rally in Tennessee, October 2011:* "It's going to be 20 feet high. It's going to have barbed wire on the top. It's going to be electrified. And there's going to be a sign on the other side saying, 'It will kill you—Warning.'"

### Steve King, on victimology:

*At a town hall meeting in 2012 where he was running for reelection:* "It started with Asians and it ended with Zeitgeist. So from A to Z. And most of them were victims groups, victimology, people that feel sorry for themselves. And they're out there recruiting our young people to be part of the group that feels sorry for themselves."

### Steve King, on immigrants, 2011:

"For everyone who's a valedictorian, there's another 100 out there who weigh 130 pounds—and they've got calves the size of cantaloupes because they've been hauling 75 pounds of marijuana across the desert." *(While John Boehner, then speaker of the House, reprimanded him, King stood by his comments.)*

---

*On immigration laws, May 22, 2012:* "You put out a beacon like the Statue of Liberty and who comes here? The most vigorous from every country that has donated legal immigrants to America. The cream of the crop. We've always had bird dogs around our place. In our family there's a black lab and white lab, a yellow lab, and my brother has a chocolate lab. Well, you go in and you look at a litter of pups, and you watch them. You watch how they play—they run around a little bit—and what do you want? You want a good bird dog, and you want one that's gonna be aggressive? Pick the one that's the friskiest, the one that's in games the most—not the one that's over there sleeping in the corner. You want a pet to sit on the couch, pick the one that's sleeping in the corner. That's—so, you get the pick of the litter, you got yourself a pretty good bird dog. We got the pick of every donor civilization on the planet because it's hard to get here; you had to be inspired to come. We got the vigor from the planet to come to America. Whichever generation it was, and then we taught our children that same thing."

----

*August 1, 2012, after proposing a bill to only let the government communicate in English:* "One of the great things about America is we've been unified by a common language. That common language, of course, is English. Our language is getting subdivided by some forces of the federal government. It is time to speak with a common voice. The argument that diversity is our strength has really never been backed up by logic. Its unity is where our strength is. Our Founding Fathers understood that. Modern-day multiculturalists are defying that."

----

"We could also electrify this wire (on the border) with the kind of current that would not kill somebody, but it would simply be a discouragement for them to be fooling around with it. We do that with livestock all the time." *(July 13, 2006)*

### Steve King, defending himself from being called anti-immigrant:

*In a statement to Newsmax, July 13, 2013, after making several anti-immigrant statements:* "There isn't anyone that can fairly characterize me as anti-immigrant. That's a label that the open borders people have tossed around. They're conflating the terms anti-illegal immigrant and anti-immigrant as if it were the terms *health care* and *health insurance*."

----

*After John Boehner and Eric Cantor decried remarks he made about Hispanic immigrants (see the cantaloupe quote):* "My colleagues are standing by me. They come up to me constantly and talk to me and say, you're right, I know you're right. Is the description such that they have to go out to the press and do a press conference or can they come and tell me, I know you're right, I support you? They can do that privately." *(July 27, 2013)*

### Rich Iott (R-OH) on dressing as a Nazi:

*Explaining why he participated in Nazi reenactments as part of a group that calls itself Wiking, and wore a German Waffen-SS uniform, he said:* "I've always been fascinated by the fact that here was a relatively small country that from a strictly military point of view accomplished incredible things." *(interview with the* Atlantic, *October 2010)*

### Democrats blaming video games for violence:

"These games teach a child to enjoy inflicting torture." *(Sen. Joe Lieberman [D-CT], December 9, 1993)*

———

"*Grand Theft Auto* . . . encourages [children] to have sex with prostitutes and then murder them." *(Sen. Hillary Clinton (D-NY) July 14, 2005, talking about a game that is NOT FOR KIDS!!!!)*

### On immigrants having kids here:

*David Vitter (R-LA), March 11, 2015, arguing to deny citizenship to some people born here because their parents are undocumented immigrants:* "There is a whole industry, an underworld that is selling so-called birth tourism. This acts as a magnet—a potent, powerful magnet growing in power by the year to lure more and more folks to come across the border in specific cases to have their babies here, 300,000 to 400,000 per year."

———————

*Senator Harry Reid, in a statement made on the US Senate floor in 1993 in favor of his bill, the Immigrant Stabilization Act, which would've ended birthright citizenship in the US:* "If making it easy to be an illegal alien is not enough, how about offering a reward for being an illegal immigrant? No sane country would do that, right? Guess again. If you break our laws by entering this country without permission and give birth to a child, we reward that child with US citizenship and guarantee full access to all public and social services this society provides. And that is a lot of services. Is it any wonder that two-thirds of the babies born at taxpayer expense in county-run hospitals in Los Angeles are born to illegal alien mothers?"

### Newt Gingrich, saying that secular Atheism and Islam are the same thing:

"I am convinced that if we do not decisively win the struggle over the nature of America, by the time [my grandchildren are] my age they will be in a secular atheist country, potentially one dominated by radical Islamists and with no understanding of what it once meant to be an American." *(October 21, 2010)*

### Jody Hice, describing how the Arab Spring was part of a plot to destroy America in It's Now or Never: A Call to Reclaim America, 2012 (This book again!):

"The plot had already completed three steps, and its instigators were beginning Phase Four."

### Scott Walker, on ISIS and protesters:

"If I can take on a hundred thousand protesters, I can do the same across the world." *(February 26, 2015)*

### Tea Party–backed Texas GOP congressional candidate Stephen Broden, on political revolution:

*In an interview with Dallas's WFAA-TV, October 21, 2010, suggesting the violent overthrow of the US government if Republicans don't win at the ballot box:* "Our nation was founded on violence. The option is on the table. I don't think that we should ever remove anything from the table as it relates to our liberties and our freedoms."

### KKK politician, on the media:

*David Duke ([R-LA], also Grand Dragon of the KKK) in the* Crusader, *a KKK periodical, November 1978:* "Our clear goal must be the advancement of the white race and separation of the white and black races. This goal must include freeing of the American media and government from subservient Jewish interests."

### Donald Trump, on David Duke:

*When asked about David Duke's (Grand Wizard of the KKK) endorsement of him as president:* "Well just so you understand, I don't know anything about David Duke. Ok? I don't know anything about what you're even talking about with, uh, white supremacy or white supremacists. Honestly, I don't know David Duke, I don't believe I've ever met him, I'm pretty sure I didn't meet him, and I just don't know anything about him." *(CNN, February 28, 2016)*

### Jeb Bush, on baby-machine immigrants:

*In a speech at the Faith and Freedom Coalition Conference, June 14, 2013:* "(Immigrants) are more fertile, and they love families!"

### Rick Perry, on tequila (and stereotypes):

*While speaking before a Latino convention in Texas, June 23, 2011, bombing with a joke about tequila:* "Young Hispanics in Texas can aspire to be the next Rolando Pablos, the chairman of the Texas racing commission; maybe the next Roberto De Hoyos, who heads our economic development shop; and one of my favorites, the head of the Texas Alcoholic Beverage Commission Jose Cuevas. Is that awesome? That is the right job for that man."

### Sen. Lindsey Graham, on turning over records without a warrant:

*Praising the NSA for gathering phone records from Verizon customers, on the Senate floor, June 6, 2013:* "I'm a Verizon customer. I don't mind Verizon turning over records to the government if the government is going to make sure that they try to match up a known terrorist phone with somebody in the United States. I don't think you're talking to the terrorists. I know you're not. I know I'm not. So we don't have anything to worry about."

### Steve King, on generalizing how Jewish people vote:

*In a* Boston Herald Radio *interview, March 20, 2015:* "Here is what I don't understand. I don't understand how Jews in America can be Democrats first and Jewish second and support Israel along the line of just following their president."

### Sen. Ron Johnson (R-WI), on inner city youth:

"It's unbelievable to me that liberals, that President Obama, of course he sends his children to private school, as did Al Gore, and Bill Clinton and every other celebrated liberal. They just don't want to let those idiot inner city kids that they purport to be so supportive of . . . they just don't want to give them the same opportunity their own kids have. I think it's disgraceful."

*(July 23, 2015. Johnson later told the* Washington Post *the following Thursday that he* "meant to be sarcastic" *and reflect* "the way liberals think of inner city youth.")

### Newt Gingrich, on child labor:

*At Harvard University's Kennedy School:* "It is tragic what we do in the poorest neighborhoods, entrapping children in child laws which are truly stupid. . . . These schools should get rid of unionized janitors, have one master janitor, pay local students to take care of the school." *(November 18, 2011)*

### Hillary Clinton, on juvenile justice:

*In 1996, Clinton made this statement:* "They are not just gangs of kids anymore. They are often the kinds of kids that are called 'superpredators.' No conscience, no empathy." *(The "superpredator" theory she cited had no basis in fact, but contributed to a wave of mass-incarceration that targeted African American youth. She later said she shouldn't have said that.)*

### Donald Trump, on immigration and Mexico:

*During his presidential announcement in New York City, June 16, 2015:* "The US has become a dumping ground for everybody else's problems. . . . When Mexico sends its people, they're not sending their best. They're not sending you. They're not sending you. They're sending people that have lots of problems, and they're bringing those problems with us. They're bringing drugs. They're bringing crime. They're rapists. And some, I assume, are good people."

———

*During the first GOP debate in Cleveland, Ohio, August 6, 2015:* "Our leaders are stupid. Our politicians are stupid. And the Mexican government is much smarter, much sharper, much more cunning.

　　　　　　　　　　　Sh*t Politicians Say

And they send the bad ones over because they don't want to pay for them."

---

"Now an additional 600-700 jobs in America (2,000) being eliminated for move to Mexico- via *Hartford Courant.*" *(Twitter, February 13, 2016)*

---

*Don't forget this infamous remark, made during his announcement that he would run for president, June 16, 2015:* "I will build a great wall—and nobody builds walls better than me, believe me—and I'll build them very inexpensively. I will build a great, great wall on our southern border, and I will make Mexico pay for that wall. Mark my words."

---

"FMR PRES of Mexico, Vicente Fox horribly used the *F* word when discussing the wall. He must apologize! If I did that there would be a uproar!" *(Twitter, February 25, 2016)*

---

*Also during the first GOP debate, August 6, 2015:* "If it weren't for me you wouldn't even be talking about illegal immigration. This was not a subject on anybody's mind at my announcement, except the reporters are a very dishonest lot."

## Sen. George Allen (R-VA), ridiculing opponents:

*Ridiculing S. R. Sidarth, a twenty-year-old Virginian native of Indian descent, by using an ethnic slur referring to a type of monkey found mainly in Asia, August 11, 2006:* "This fellow here, over here with the yellow shirt, macaca, or whatever his name is. He's with my opponent. He's following us around everywhere. And it's just great. . . . Let's give a welcome to macaca, here. Welcome to America and the real world of Virginia."

### Trent Lott, on KKK members:

*At the 100th birthday celebration for Strom Thurmond, who ran on a segregationist platform for president in 1948:* "I want to say this about my state: When Strom Thurmond ran for president, we voted for him. We're proud of it. And if the rest of the country had followed our lead, we wouldn't have had all these problems over all these years, either." *(broadcast on C-SPAN December 2002)*

### Sen. Mary Landrieu (D-LA), on unemployment stereotypes:

*When asked why New Orleans Mayor Ray Nagin failed to follow the city's evacuation plan and press the buses into service on* Fox News Sunday, *September 11, 2005, this was a part of his response:* "Mayor Nagin and most mayors in this country have a hard time getting their people to work on a sunny day, let alone getting them out of the city in front of a hurricane."

### David Vitter (R-LA) (this again?!):

"When folks from other countries give birth in the US, their kids become American citizens. This should be illegal." *(Twitter, March 10, 2015)*

### Donald Trump, on Muslims celebrating 9/11:

*At a rally in Alabama, November 21, 2015:* "I watched when the World Trade Center came tumbling down. And I watched in Jersey City, New Jersey, where thousands and thousands of people were cheering as that building was coming down. Thousands of people were cheering."

*He defended the above claim to ABC's George Stephanopolous on December 2, 2015:* "It was well covered at the time, George.

Now, I know they don't like to talk about it, but it was well covered at the time. There were people over in New Jersey that were watching it, a heavy Arab population, that were cheering as the buildings came down. Not good." *(Footage did show up of people celebrating, but of about eight people, not thousands.)*

––––––––––

*Referring to himself in third person on his own Twitter, December 7, 2015:* "Donald J. Trump is calling for a total and complete shutdown of Muslims entering the United States until our country's representatives can figure out what is going on."

––––––––––

*On* Fox & Friends, *December 2, 2015:* "But we're fighting a very politically correct war. And the other thing is with the terrorists, you have to take out their families. When you get these terrorists, you have to take out their families. They care about their lives, don't kid yourself. But they say they don't care about their lives. You have to take out their families." *(If what he said were implemented, it would arguably be considered a war crime.)*

### Steve King again, on the Washington Redskins:

"Obama raids Redskins by weaponizing USPTO. Cancels Redskins logo! Free people will not tolerate a Kim Jong POTUS." *(Twitter, June 18, 2014)*

### David Vitter (R-LA), on taking away birthright citizenship:

*During hearings over anti-abortion language added to an anti–human trafficking bill, March 2015:* "As the presiding officer knows our founding fathers including our later founding fathers who came up with the language of the 14th amendment, chose their words carefully and it is a fundamental rule of either constitutional or statutory construction that any word there, any phrase there must be there for a reason. It is not there just to add extra words without adding meaning."

### Mike Huckabee, on overturned laws:

*On the* Michael Medved Show, *September 10, 2015:* "Because I've been just *drilled* by TV hosts over the past week, 'How dare you say that, uh, you know, it's not the law of the land?' Because that's their phrase, 'it's the law of the land.' Michael, the Dred Scott decision of 1857 still remains to this day the law of the land which says that black people aren't fully human. Does anybody still follow the Dred Scott Supreme Court decision?" *(Note: the Dred Scott decision was overturned by the passage of the 13th Amendment, outlawing slavery.)*

### Assuming immigration and abortion go hand-in-hand:

*Mike Huckabee, speaking to a conservative Christian group, May 20, 2011:* "Sometimes we talk about why we're importing so many people in our workforce. It might be for the last 35 years, we have aborted more than a million people who would have been in our workforce had we not had the holocaust of liberalized abortion under a flawed Supreme Court ruling in 1973."

### Charlie Rangel, explaining how he was confused by the term "white cracker," in a HuffPost Live interview, November 10, 2014:

"I thought that was a term of endearment. They're so proud of their heritage and all of the things they believe in."

### Bill Clinton, on bad wording:

*Interview with Ed Gordon on BET, November 2, 1994:* "African Americans watch the same news at night that ordinary Americans do."

### Ronald Reagan, on hunger:

*During a TV speech called "A Time for Choosing," October 27, 1964:*
"We were told four years ago that 17 million people went to bed hungry every night. Well, that was probably true. They were all on a diet."

### President George H. W. Bush, 14th Amendment?

*When asked by reporter Roger Sherman on whether or not atheists should be considered patriots, Bush replied:* "I don't know that atheists should be considered citizens, nor should they be considered patriots. This is one nation under God." *(August 27, 1988)*

### Things were a lot different back in the 1940s:

*Robert Byrd (D-WV), in a 1947 letter to a Grand Wizard of the KKK:* "The Klan is needed today as never before, and I am anxious to see its rebirth here in West Virginia."

### Pat Buchanan, on segregation:

*Commenting on race relations in the 1940s and 1950s:* "There were no politics to polarize us then, to magnify every slight. The 'Negroes' of Washington had their public schools, restaurants, bars, movie houses, playgrounds and churches; and we had ours." *(taken from Right from the Beginning, his 1988 autobiography)*

### And finally, David Vitter, after stereotyping Mexicans during a debate for the Louisiana senate seat between Vitter and Rep. Charlie Melancon (D-LA), October 28, 2010:

MODERATOR: Do you offer them an apology or do you stand by the ad?

VITTER: We have an illegal immigration problem and a huge part of that is the Mexican border. That is a fact, that is not a stereotype.

Ninety-seven percent of our apprehensions of illegals is at the Mexican border. That is a fact, that is not a stereotype. Over 80 percent of the 12-15 million illegals in this country have come through that border from Mexico and South American countries. That is a fact, that is not a stereotype. Now there's one thing in that ad that is offensive and that is Mister Melancon's votes that the ad highlights. [. . .]

MODERATOR: How do you respond to the Hispanic Chamber of Commerce, the Catholic Charities, the Archdiocese of New Orleans who say that this ad played into offensive racial stereotypes?

VITTER: Let me just ask you, what is the stereotype?

MODERATOR: They're talking about the images seen in your ad.

VITTER: Is it a stereotype that folks coming across the border—that is a problem and they look like that? Dennis that is a fact, that is not a stereotype! Let's get our heads out of the sand!

# Chapter 11

# *Sh\*t Politicians Say About Women*

I love women, I really do. But from women's rights to scandals, politicians have a long history of being jerks to women. Cases in point:

### Todd Akin, on human anatomy(?):

*First said in a local news interview, August 19, 2012; mocked and derided since:* "If it's a legitimate rape, the female body has ways to try to shut that whole thing down."

### Christine O'Donnell, on women in the military:

"By integrating women into particularly military institutes, it cripples the readiness of our defense. Schools like The Citadel train young men to confidently lead other young men into a battlefield where one of them will die. And when you have women in that situation, it creates a whole new set of dynamics which are distracting to training these men to kill or be killed." *(During a 1995 C-SPAN interview)*

### Pat Buchanan, on women then:

*In a column called "Feminism and Futility," 1983:* "Rail as they will about 'discrimination,' women are simply not endowed by nature with the same measures of single-minded ambition and the will to succeed in the fiercely competitive world of Western capitalism."

### Donald Trump, on women now:

*On Carly Fiorina's face,* Rolling Stone *interview, September 2015:* "Look at that face! Would anyone vote for that? Can you imagine that, the face of our next president?! I mean, she's a woman, and I'm not s'posedta say bad things, but really, folks, come on. Are we serious?"

---

"If Hillary Clinton can't satisfy her husband what makes her think she can satisfy America?" *(Twitter, on April 16, 2015)*

### And the binders full of women:

*Mitt Romney, on staffing his cabinet as governor of Massachusetts:* "I went to a number of women's groups and said, 'Can you help us find folks?' and they brought us whole binders full of women." *(during the second presidential debate, October 15, 2012)*

### Jody Hice, on abortion and genocide:

*Waxing poetic in his book,* It's Now or Never: A Call to Reclaim America, *2012 (a book apparently full of stupid—I've quoted it at least a half-dozen times in the last chapter!):* "How many times have we denounced the murderous acts of people like Hitler? Most certainly, his actions and similar ones by other political leaders should be vehemently condemned! Yet, we so easily overlook the genocide that has been committed within our own country. Our murderous dealings are much worse than Hitler's six million Jews or Mussolini's three hundred thousand. The genocide in America is inexcusable! It is worse than genocide. We are guilty of eugenics!"

### Terri Lynn Land, on equal pay for women:

*In a speech at the Community House, Bloomfield Township, Michigan, 2010:* "Well we all like to be paid more and that's great but the reality is that women have a different lifestyle. They have kids, they have to take them to get dentist appointments, doctors' appointments, all those kinds of things and they're more interested in flexibility in a job than pay."

---

*Her clarification regarding the above,* Wall Street Journal, *April 12, 2014:* "I support equal pay as a woman, of course, as a woman employer—twice as local county clerk and as secretary of state. But I think flexibility is important, too."

### Donald Trump, on planned parenthood:

*After saying he would defund Planned Parenthood earlier in his campaign:* "As far as Planned Parenthood is concerned, I'm pro-life, I'm totally against abortion having to do with Planned Parenthood. But millions and millions of women, cervical cancer, breast cancer, are helped by Planned Parenthood. So you can say whatever you want but they have millions of women going through Planned Parenthood that are helped greatly." *(Republican debate in Texas, February 26, 2016)*

---

*In an interview with Chris Matthews, March 30, 2016, Trump said that "there would have to be some punishment" for women who seek abortions, if abortions are outlawed. Three hours later, he changed his position in a press release due to the backlash, saying:* "The woman is a victim in this case, as is the life in her womb."

### Chuck Winder, implying women use rape as an excuse for abortions:

*Sponsoring a forced ultrasound bill in a senate hearing, March 20, 2012:* "I would hope that when a woman goes in to a physician with a rape issue, that physician will indeed ask her about perhaps her marriage, was this pregnancy caused by normal relations in a marriage or was it truly caused by a rape."

### On being "pro-life":

*Rick Santorum on CNN's* Pierce Morgan Tonight, *January 20, 2012, stating his position on abortions in the case of rape and incest:* "I think the right approach is to accept this horribly created—in the sense of rape—but nevertheless a gift in a very broken way, the gift of human life, and accept what God has given to you. . . . [Rape victims should] make the best of a bad situation."

———

*Paul Ryan, referring to rape as a "method of conception" when asked if it should it be legal for a woman to be able to get an abortion if she's raped:* "I'm very proud of my pro-life record, and I've always adopted the idea that, the position that the method of conception doesn't change the definition of life." *(In an interview with WJHL, Roanoake, Virginia, August 2011)*

———

*Indiana Republican Senate candidate and treasurer Richard Mourdock, during a US Senate debate, October 23, 2012:* "And I think even when life begins in that horrible situation of rape, that it is something that God intended to happen."

### Newt Gingrich, on cheating:

*The Newtster, in March 2011, speaking about his many affairs:* "There's no question at times of my life, partially driven by how passionately I felt about this country, that I worked far too hard and things happened in my life that were not appropriate. And what I can tell you is that when I did things that were wrong, I wasn't trapped in situation ethics, I was doing things that were wrong, and yet, I was doing them."

### Carly Fiorina, on contraception access:

"We are not waging a war on women simply because we believe there is no good reason for birth control to be free." *(Conservative Political Action Conference [CPAC], 2014)*

### Mark Warden (R-NH), on abusive relationships:

*On February 26, 2013, during a state House Criminal Justice and Public Safety Committee on legislation making domestic violence a felony rather than a misdemeanor, Warden argued against abusive relationships:* "Some people could make the argument that a lot of people like being in abusive relationships. It's a love-hate relationship. It's very, very common for people to stick around with somebody they love who also abuses him or her. . . . Is the solution to those kind of dysfunctional relationships going to be more government, another law? I'd say no. People are always free to leave." *(He later told the* Concord Monitor, *where the story was first printed, that his statements were taken out of context.)*

### On ugly women (or one particular one, anyway):

"Does anyone not believe that Congressman Annie Kuster is as ugly as sin? And I hope I haven't offended sin." *(Steve Vaillancourt (R-NH) October 13, 2014,* NH Insider)

### BERNIE?! Is that YOU?!:

*Bernie Sanders, in his 30s at the time and just beginning to run for (and yet to win) political office for the Liberty Union party, was full of, shall we say, radical ideas. He wrote an essay in 1972 for the alternative rag* Vermont Freeman. *Here's an excerpt from what has been described as a stream-of-consciousness essay on the nature of male-female sexual dynamics:* "A man goes home and masturbates his typical fantasy. A woman on her knees, a woman tied up, a woman abused. A woman enjoys intercourse with her man—as she fantasizes being raped by three men simultaneously." *(The rest of the essay is somewhat tamer, explaining his ideas about gender roles. His presidential campaign has tried to put some distance between this essay and the Bernie of today—but it's all true!)*

### Former Sen. John Edwards, on having an affair:

*In an ABC News interview with Bob Woodruff, August 8, 2008, after Edwards was caught cheating on his wife:* "Can I explain to you what happened? First of all it happened during a period after she was in remission from cancer." *(Ouch!!!)*

### Mitt Romney, and his varying views on abortion:

*In the campaign against Ted Kennedy for Massachusetts Senator, 1994:* "I believe that since *Roe v. Wade* has been the law for 20 years, it should be sustained and supported. And I sustain and support that law and support the right of a woman to make that choice."

———

*And in his 2002 campaign for governor:* "I will preserve and protect a woman's right to choose and am devoted and dedicated to honoring my word in that regard."

———

*In an op-ed for* National Review, *June 18, 2011, outlining three policies he supports which contradict the above:* "I am pro-life and believe that abortion should be limited to only instances of rape, incest, or to save the life of the mother. I support the reversal of *Roe v. Wade*, because it is bad law and bad medicine. *Roe* was a misguided ruling that was a result of a small group of activist federal judges legislating from the bench. I support the Hyde Amendment, which broadly bars the use of federal funds for abortions. And as president, I will support efforts to prohibit federal funding for any organization like Planned Parenthood, which primarily performs abortions or offers abortion-related services.

"I will reinstate the Mexico City Policy to ensure that nongovernmental organizations that receive funding from America refrain from performing or promoting abortion services as a method of family planning, in other countries. This includes ending American funding for any United Nations or other foreign assistance program that promotes or performs abortions on women around the world.

"I will advocate for and support a Pain-Capable Unborn Child Protection Act to protect unborn children who are capable of feeling pain from abortion. And perhaps most importantly, I will only appoint judges who adhere to the Constitution and the laws as they are written, not as they want them to be written."

### Tom Patton, Ohio State Senator Majority Leader, on gals ("gals"? really??):

"The gal that's running against me is a 30-year-old, you know, mom, mother of two infants, and I don't know if anybody explained to her we've got to spend three nights a week in Columbus. So, how does that work out for you? I waited until I was 48 and my kids were raised and at least adults before we took the opportunity to try." *(Speaking about his opponent on January 28, 2016. He has since apologized, but still—stupid thing to say.)*

### State Rep. Mike Duvall (R-CA), caught on tape:

"She wears little eye-patch underwear. So, the other day she came here with her underwear, Thursday. And so, we had made love Wednesday—a lot! And so she'll, she's all, 'I am going up and down the stairs, and you're dripping out of me!' So messy!" *(On a live mic referring to an affair with a lobbyist, September 9, 2009. Mikey resigned after his sex comments were broadcast.)*

### Chris Christie, to an occupy protester:

"You know, something may be going down tonight, but it ain't going to be jobs, sweetheart." *(January 8, 2012)*

### Jeb Bush, on Supergirl:

*When asked who his favorite superhero is during a campaign event in Las Vegas:* "I saw that *Supergirl* is on TV. I saw it when I was working out this morning, there was an ad promoting *Supergirl*. She looked pretty hot. I don't know what channel it's on, but I'm looking forward to that. . . ." *(October 21, 2015)*

### Rep. Steve King, on child rape:

*Making a bizarre antichoice argument in August 2012:* "[A man could rape a thirteen-year-old], take that girl off the playground, haul her across a state line, force her to get an abortion to eradicate the evidence of his crime, and bring her back and drop her off at the swing set. And that's not against the law in the United States."

———

*Three weeks after making the rapist at the swing set remark above:* "Well I just haven't heard of that being a circumstance that's been brought to me in any personal way, and I'd be open to discussion about that subject matter."

### On rape:

*David Brooks on* Meet the Press, *addressing the Penn State rape case, November 15, 2011:* "I don't think it was just a Penn State problem. You know, you spend 30 or 40 years muddying the moral waters here. We have lost our clear sense of what evil is, what sin is; and so, when people see things like that, they don't have categories to put it into. They vaguely know it's wrong, but they've been raised in a morality that says, "If it feels all right for you, it's probably OK."

---

*Roger Rivard (R-WI), commenting in October 2012 on a case where a high school student sexually assaulted a younger student in the band room:* "Some girls rape easy." *(He said his comments were taken out of context, and he lost reelection to Democrat Stephen Smith the following November.)*

---

*Pete Nielsen (R-ID) during an Idaho State House hearing, February 25, 2016, about proposed antichoice legislation:* "Now, I'm of the understanding that in many cases of rape it does not involve any pregnancy because of the trauma of the situation. That may be true with incest a little bit."

### Rick Santorum, on contraception:

*Santorum, in an interview with a blogger in October 2011 about his opinion of contraception:* "One of the things I will talk about, that no president has talked about before, is I think the dangers of contraception in this country. It's not okay. It's a license to do things in a sexual realm that is counter to how things are supposed to be. [Sex] is supposed to be within marriage. It's supposed to be for purposes that are yes, conjugal . . . but also procreative. That's the perfect way that a sexual union should happen. . . . This is special and it needs to be seen as special."

### On where fetuses grow:

*Sue Swayze, director of Indiana's Right to Life, defending an ultrasound bill, February 21, 2013:* "I got pregnant vaginally. Something else could come in my vagina for a medical test that wouldn't be

that intrusive to me. So I find that argument a little ridiculous."
*(Note: fetuses do not and cannot grow in vaginas.)*

### Rep. Bob Dornan (R-CA), on male feminists:

*At an anti-abortion rally in Washington DC, February 1990:* "Men in the pro-choice movement are either men trapped in women's bodies . . . or younger guys who are like camp followers looking for easy sex."

### On women cooking:

*Poster issued by MLA Rick Strankman to promote a pie auction fundraiser, April 2015:* "Bring Your Wife's Pie." *(The poster was taken down after sparking the ire of feminists.)*

### Maybe this is why women aren't voting for you:

*Jeb Bush, during his failed 1994 Florida gubernatorial campaign:* "[Women on welfare] should be able to get their lives together and find a husband."

———

*Ben Carson, explaining his anti-choice stance using sexist rhetoric, October 11, 2013:* "There is no war on them (women), the war is on their babies. What we need to do is reeducate the women to understand that they are the defenders of these babies."

———

*Jeb Bush, on Bill Bennett's radio show* Morning in America, *August 2015:* "If people are bringing . . . pregnant women are coming in to have babies simply because they can do it, then there ought to be greater enforcement. [We need] better enforcement so that you don't have these, you know, 'anchor babies,' as they're described, coming into the country."

Sh*t Politicians Say

### On women's bodies:

*Texas state Rep. Jodie Laubenberg, on why there shouldn't be a rape or incest exception in Texas's sweeping anti-choice bills, June 24, 2013:* "In the emergency room they have what's called rape kits where a woman can get cleaned out."

### On pro-choice slogans:

*Michele Bachmann (R-MN), missed the irony of using a pro-choice slogan on the* Sean Hannity Show, *August 20, 2009:* "That's why people need to continue to go to the town halls, continue to melt the phone lines of their liberal members of Congress, and let them know, under no certain circumstances will I give the government control over my body and my health care decisions."

### On women for vice president:

*Rep. Pat Schroeder, on why George H. W. Bush was unlikely to choose a woman as his running mate in 1988:* "People would say, 'We need a man on the ticket.'"

### Nikki Haley, on birth control access:

*The Republican governor from South Carolina, on* The View, *April 3, 2012, defending her anti-contraception policies by saying:* "Women don't care about contraception."

### Gov. Bobby Jindal, on criminalizing women who get abortions:

*After signing anti-choice legislation in Louisiana, he made the comparison to women seeking abortions to criminals being arrested:* "When officers arrest criminals today, they are read their rights. Now if we're giving criminals their basic rights and they have to be informed of those rights, it seems to me only common sense we would have to do the same thing for women before they make the choice about whether to get an abortion." *(July 7, 2011)*

### John Kasich, on housewives "venturing out":

*At a town hall meeting, Fairfax, Virginia, February 22, 2016:* "How did I get elected? Nobody was—I didn't have anybody for me. We just got an army of people and many women who left their kitchens to go out and go door to door and put yard signs up for me. All the way back, when things were different. Now you call homes, and everybody's working."

### Donald Trump, on women (his greatest hits):

*On why Megyn Kelly was "hostile" to him during the first GOP debate:* "She gets out and she starts asking me all sorts of ridiculous questions. You could see that she had blood coming out of her eyes, blood coming out of her . . . wherever. In my opinion, she was off-base." *(From August 7, 2015. This quote got him banned from NBC.)*

———

*On the* O'Reilly Factor, *May 29, 2007, discussing Rosie O'Donnell when she left* The View: "She went to my wedding, she had lots and lots of cake, and I'll tell you what, she's a terrible human being."

———

*From his book* Trump: How to Get Rich, *2004:* "All of the women on *The Apprentice* flirted with me—consciously or unconsciously. That's to be expected."

———

"You know, it really doesn`t matter what [the media] write as long as you`ve got a young and beautiful piece of ass." *(interview with* Esquire *magazine, 1991)*

———

"26,000 unreported sexual assaults in the military-only 238 convictions. What did these geniuses expect when they put men & women together?" *(Twitter, May 7, 2013)*

———

"While Bette Midler is an extremely unattractive woman, I refuse to say that because I always insist on being politically correct." *(Twitter, October 28, 2012)*

———

*In an interview with* Rolling Stone, *September 2015, when asked how he would react if his daughter Ivanka posed for* Playboy: "I don't think Ivanka would do that, although she does have a very nice figure. I've said if Ivanka weren't my daughter, perhaps I'd be dating her."

### Rep. Trent Franks (R-AZ), on rape and pregnancy:

*Judiciary Committee meeting, June 12 2013, on a federal twenty-week abortion ban:* "Before . . . my friends on the left side of the aisle here tried to make rape and incest the subject —because, you know, the incidence of rape resulting in pregnancy are very low." *(Note: studies show that pregnancy from rape is more likely than pregnancy from consensual sex.)*

### Mike Huckabee, on contraception:

*At the RNC Winter Meeting, January 23, 2014:* "And if the Democrats want to insult the women of America by making them believe that they are helpless without Uncle Sugar coming in and providing for them a prescription each month for birth control because they cannot control their libido or their reproductive system without the help of government then so be it!"

### Marco Rubio, on Planned Parenthood:

*Interview with KCCI, on the debunked footage of PP employees selling fetal tissue, September 21, 2015:* "I just think you've created an industry now—a situation where very much, you've created an incentive for people not just to look forward to having more abortions, but being able to sell that fetal tissue—these centers—for purposes of making a profit off it, as you've seen in some of these Planned Parenthood affiliates."

### On the war on women:

*Rand Paul, not realizing most women aren't related to him, nor are becoming doctors and lawyers, on NBC's* Meet the Press, *January 6, 2014:* "I'm scratching my head because if there was a war on women, I think they won. You know, the women in my family are incredibly successful. I have a niece at Cornell vet school, and 85 percent of the young people there are women. In law school, 60 percent are women; in med school, 55 percent. My younger sister's an ob-gyn with six kids and doing great. You know, I don't see so much that women are downtrodden; I see women rising up and doing great things."

### Jody Hice, on women in politics:

"If the woman's within the authority of her husband, I don't see a problem." *(In the Athens* Banner-Herald, *2004.)*

### Mike Huckabee, on Beyoncé:

"Beyoncé is incredibly talented—gifted, in fact. She has an exceptional set of pipes and can actually sing. She is a terrific dancer – without the explicit moves best left for the privacy of her bedroom. Jay Z is a very shrewd businessman, but I wonder: Does it occur to him that he is arguably crossing the line from husband to pimp by exploiting his wife as a sex object?" *(From his book* God, Guns, Grits and Gravy, *October 11, 2014)*

### Finally, here's Jimmy Carter, on bad thoughts:

"I've looked on many women with lust. I've committed adultery in my heart many times. God knows I will do this and forgives me." *(In an interview with* Playboy *one month prior to the 1976 election.)*

# Chapter 12

# *Sh\*t Politicians Say About Religion*

As I've said before, I think religion is a crutch for the weak, and it baffles me why so many American politicians lean on it. Is it to excite their base? Is it to not catch cooties, since anyone who says anything bad about religion is treated as some sort of pariah on the political field (I should know)? Whatever the reason, it's all stupid, and that's why it deserves its own chapter. Here's the dumbest stuff politicians have said about religion.

### On America's future:

*Rep. John Fleming (R-LA) speaking to the Republican Women of Bossier group, August 26, 2010:* "We have two competing world views here and there is no way that we can reach across the aisle—one is going to have to win. . . . We are either going to go down the socialist road and become like Western Europe and create, I guess really a godless society, an atheist society. Or we're going to continue down the other pathway where we believe in freedom of speech, individual liberties and that we remain a Christian nation. . . . So we're going to have to solve that argument before we can once again reach across and work together on things."

### Mike Huckabee, on WWJD:

"Jesus was too smart to ever run for public office . . . that's what Jesus would do." *(November 28, 2007)*

### George Bush Sr. cares:

*President George H. W. Bush, speaking to employees of an insurance company during the 1992 New Hampshire primary:* "You cannot be president of the United States if you don't have faith. Remember Lincoln, going to his knees in times of trial and the Civil War and all that stuff? You can't be. And we are blessed. So don't feel sorry for—don't cry for me, Argentina. Message: I care." *(Why am I picturing Dana Carvey saying this in his Bush voice?!)*

### Down with masturbation!:

*Christine O'Donnell, advocating against masturbation in a 1996 appearance on MTV's* Sex in The 90s *TV show:* "It is not enough to be abstinent with other people, you also have to be abstinent alone. The Bible says that lust in your heart is committing adultery. You can't masturbate without lust!"

### Rick Perry, on austerity:

*During an appearance on James Robinson's TV show* Life Today, *June 2011, Perry threw together word salad to explain the link between the Bible and economic austerity:* "I think in America from time to time we have to go through some difficult times—and I think we're going through those difficult economic times for a purpose, to bring us back to those Biblical principles of you know, you don't spend all the money. You work hard for those six years and you put up that seventh year in the warehouse to take you through the hard times. And not spending all of our money. Not asking for Pharaoh to give everything to everybody and to take care of folks because at the end of the day, it's slavery. We become slaves to government."

### On public education:

*Presidential candidate Pat Buchanan addressing an anti-gay rally in Des Moines, Iowa, February 11, 1996:* "We're going to bring back

God and the Bible and drive the gods of secular humanism right out of the public schools of America."

### Huckabee, pining for televangelists:

*Mike Huckabee, at the Rediscover God in America conference, March 4, 2011:* "I almost wish that there would be, like, a simultaneous telecast, and all Americans would be forced—forced at gunpoint no less—to listen to every David Barton message, and I think our country would be better for it. I wish it'd happen."

### On kicking God out of schools:

*Christine O'Donnell, on Bill Maher's* Politically Incorrect, *August 1998:* "We took the Bible and prayer out of public schools. Now we're having weekly shootings. We had the 60s sexual revolution, and now people are dying of AIDS."

---

*Jody Hice, from his radio show after the Sandy Hook massacre, December 2012:* "We have tragedies, horrifying tragedies such as this, happening in America today with much greater frequency because God is largely removed from our culture . . . we have been kicking God out of the schools, and we have been kicking God out of the public square."

### What Is Obama up to in Indonesia (the country with the highest percentage of Muslims in the world)?:

*Rick Santorum, Fox News interview, May 2010:* "I think the Democrats are actually worried he [Obama] may go to Indonesia and bow to more Muslims."

### On the wrath of God:

*Bobby Jindal at a prayer rally, December 10, 2014:* "We have watched sin escalate to a proportion the nation has never seen before.

We live in the first generation in which . . . homosexuality has been embraced. . . . While the United States still claims to be a nation 'under God' it is obvious that we have greatly strayed from our foundations in Christianity. This year we have seen a dramatic increase in tornadoes that have taken the lives of many . . . and let us not forget that we are only six years from the tragic events of Hurricane Katrina."

## On the Islamization of America:

*Mike Huckabee, in an op-ed piece he wrote for Fox News, November 23, 2015:* "After this attack in West Africa, Obama's new domestic terrorism plan probably requires Americans to memorize Koran verses."

## Donald Trump, on honesty:

"How can Ted Cruz be an Evangelical Christian when he lies so much and is so dishonest?" *(Twitter, February 12, 2016)*

## Donald Trump, on religion:

*Donald Trump, flubbing the Bible at Liberty University, January 19, 2016:* "Two Corinthians, 3:17, that's the whole ballgame. 'Where the Spirit of the Lord is, right? Where the spirit of the Lord is, there is liberty.'" *(It's "Second Corinthians.")*

———

*Explaining his "Two Corinthians" flub:* "Tony Perkins wrote that out for me. He knew I was going to Liberty, and he has a great respect for Liberty, and he is a very, very good guy. And he wrote out the number 'Two' Corinthians, which I could show you very nicely, if you like." *(January 21, 2016)*

### Preventing tragedy:

*Rick Perry's statement, January 16, 2013, in response to Obama's gun control proposals in the wake of the Sandy Hook massacre:* "No gun law could've saved the children of Sandy Hook Elementary. . . . Laws, the only redoubt of secularism, will not suffice. Let us all return to our places of worship and pray for help."

### Tony Perkins, on Islam:

*"How do you Solve a Problem like Sharia," an email from Tony Perkins to the Family Research Council, December 9, 2015:* "What most people either don't realize or willfully ignore is that only 16 percent of Islam is a religion—the rest is a combination of military, judicial, economic, and political system. Christianity, by comparison, isn't a judicial or economic code—but a faith. So to suggest that we would be imposing some sort of religious test on Muslims is inaccurate. Sharia is not a religion in the context of the First Amendment."

### Tod Cruz, on chaplains and atheists:

*Speaking at the Network of Iowa Christian Home Educators, March 18, 2014:* "It is the job of a chaplain to be insensitive to atheists."

### Someone wants to be Emperor Palpatine:

*Randall Terry, the News Sentinel, Ft. Wayne, Indiana, August 16, 1993:* "I want you to just let a wave of intolerance wash over you. I want you to let a wave of hatred wash over you. Yes, hate is good . . . Our goal is a Christian nation. We have a biblical duty, we are called on by God to conquer this country. We don't want equal time. We don't want pluralism."

### On pagans infiltrating churches:

*Randall Terry, Operation Rescue, speech in Jackson, Mississippi, April 1992:* "What this is coming down to is who runs the country. It's us against them. It's the good guys versus the bad guys. It's the God-fearing people against the pagans, and some of the pagans are going to church."

### Creationism, à la Christine O'Donnell:

*Christine O'Donnell, appearing on* Politically Incorrect, *unaired, but recorded October 15, 1998:* "You know what, evolution is a myth. . . . Why aren't monkeys still evolving into humans?" *(Re-aired on* Real Time with Bill Maher, *September 24, 2010)*

---

*Michele Bachmann, in the* Stillwater Gazette, *2011:* "Where do we say that a cell became a blade of grass, which became a starfish, which became a cat, which became a donkey, which became a human being? There's a real lack of evidence from change from actual species to a different type of species. That's where it's difficult to prove."

### Pat Buchanan and what Obama's really up to:

"Obama's White House thus enlisted in the long and successful campaign to expel Christianity from the public square, diminish its presence in our public life, and reduce its role to that of just another religion." *(from* Suicide of a Superpower, *2011)*

### Ben Carson, on the purpose of the pyramids:

*Ben Carson's 1998 graduation key-note address:* "My own personal theory is that Joseph built the pyramids to store grain. Now all the archaeologists think that they were made for the pharaohs' graves.

But, you know, it would have to be something awfully big if you stop and think about it. And I don't think it'd just disappear over the course of time to store that much grain." *(Film resurfaced November 5, 2015, via the* Washington Post*)*

### Mike Huckabee, politics for Jesus:

*At the National Pastors' Conference, 1998:* "I didn't get into politics because I thought government had a better answer. I got into politics because I knew government didn't have the real answers, that the real answers lie in accepting Jesus Christ into our lives."

### Michele Bachmann, not even close:

"There are hundreds and hundreds of scientists, many of them holding Nobel Prizes, who believe in intelligent design." *(speaking to the League of Women Voters in 2006)*

### I'm not familiar with this passage in the Bible (from MSNBC, interview with Martin Bashir and Rep. Joe Barton [R-TX], May 9, 2012):

BASHIR: How do you square your approach with the Psalm 146, where the Psalmist writes this: "He gives food to the hungry. The lord protects foreigners. He defends orphans and widows." Isn't this the exact opposite of the cuts being proposed by Republicans in Congress?

BARTON: No, the lord helps those who helps themselves . . .

BASHIR: Which verse of scripture is that, sir?

BARTON: Well, it's uh . . .

BASHIR: I don't think you'll find that in the Old or New Testament.

BARTON: Well, that was taught to me by my father who is president of the United Methodist school board in Waco, Texas, and Bryan, Texas.

### The old "Pope is the antichrist" thing:

*Rep. Susan DeLemus (R-NH), on* February 22, 2016, *responding to a Facebook status where she said,* "The Pope is the antichrist": "I was actually referencing the papacy. And what I wrote after that 'do your research,' if you read the Geneva Bible, which is the Bible I use when we study, the commentary is—actually by the founders of the United States actually, the Protestant Church— their commentary references the papacy as the anti-Christ. And I think actually in one part of it, and I don't remember who it was that wrote it, there was one of the popes that they had referenced as the anti-Christ. So that's all I was referring to, the papacy, not particularly that one particular pope because the papacy is a seat. It's not just one person."

### Getting fired over bigotry:

*Bob FitzSimmonds (R-VA), former treasurer of the Virginia Republican Party, posted this on Facebook in 2014:* "Exactly what part of our nation's fabric was woven by Muslims? What about Sikhs, Animists, and Jainists? Should we be thanking them too?" *(The backlash was so strong he was forced to resign.)*

### On the way the judicial system works:

*Rev. Jody Hice, pastor of Bethlehem First Baptist Church and president of Ten Commandments-Georgia Inc, at a rally, November 23, 2003:* "We are no longer going to tolerate the continual assault on our God, our faith and our freedom by . . . these judges of tyranny. We need to send a message—we are sick and tired of our freedoms being hijacked by judicial terrorists."

### She's not a witch, she's you:

*Delaware GOP Senate candidate Christine O'Donnell, in a 1999 unaired appearance on Bill Maher's* Politically Incorrect: "I dabbled into witchcraft—I never joined a coven. But I did, I did . . . I dabbled into witchcraft. I hung around people who were doing these things. I'm not making this stuff up. I know what they told me they do. . . . One of my first dates with a witch was on a satanic altar, and I didn't know it. I mean, there's little blood there and stuff like that. We went to a movie and then had a midnight picnic on a satanic altar." *(Maher re-aired it in 2010 on* Real Time with Bill Maher.*)*

### We're back in the Dark Ages:

*Rep. Steve King (R-IA), in an interview with Glenn Beck, March 18, 2010, on Congress voting on the health-care bill:* "They intend to vote on the Sabbath, during Lent, to take away the liberty that we have right from God. This is an affront to God."

### On how old Earth is:

*Marco Rubio, when asked by* GQ *magazine in November 2012 how old he thought the earth was:* "I'm not a scientist, man. I can tell you what recorded history says, I can tell you what the Bible says, but I think that's a dispute amongst theologians and I think it has nothing to do with the gross domestic product or economic growth of the United States. I think the age of the universe has zero to do with how our economy is going to grow. I'm not a scientist. I don't think I'm qualified to answer a question like that. At the end of the day, I think there are multiple theories out there on how the universe was created and I think this is a country where people should have the opportunity to teach them all. I think parents should be able to teach their kids what their faith says, what science says. Whether the Earth was created in seven days, or seven actual eras, I'm not sure we'll ever be able to answer that. It's one of the great mysteries.

**Presidents can't amend the Constitution by themselves (it's a process that involves congress and the states):**

*Mike Huckabee, trying to appeal to Republican primary voters in Michigan in 2008:* "[Some of my opponents] do not want to change the Constitution, but I believe it's a lot easier to change the Constitution than it would be to change the word of the living God, and that's what we need to do is to amend the Constitution so it's in God's standards rather than try to change God's standards."

———

*Mike Huckabee, after winning Kansas, February 9, 2008 (and the Associated Press called Louisiana in his favor):* "I didn't major in math. I majored in miracles, and I still believe in them, too."

**On church and state:**

*Glen Urquhart, the Tea Party–backed Republican nominee for the Delaware House seat held by Rep. Mike Castle, in April 2010 said:* "Do you know, where does this phrase 'separation of church and state' come[s] from? It was not in Jefferson's letter to the Danbury Baptists. . . . The exact phrase 'separation of Church and State' came out of Adolph Hitler's mouth, that's where it comes from. So the next time your liberal friends talk about the separation of Church and State, ask them why they're Nazis."

**And finally, Santorum checked in on the Crusades:**

*Rick Santorum, campaigning for president in South Carolina, February 2011:* "The idea that the Crusades and the fight of Christendom against Islam is somehow an aggression on our part is absolutely antihistorical. And that is what the perception is by the American Left who hates Christendom. . . . What I'm talking about is onward American soldiers. What we're talking about are core American values."

# Chapter 13

# Sh*t George W. Bush (and His Administration) Said

"Just to get you on the record, where does the buck stop in this administration?" —White House reporter

"The President." —White House Press Secretary Scott McClellan, during a conference about Hurricane Katrina September 6, 2005

"George W. Bush did an incredible job in the presidency, defending us from freedom." —Rick Perry in 2010

It's no secret I hate these guys. So to include a chapter with mostly Bushisms, some stuff he and his administration said, along with the morons that mishandled Katrina, is a great privilege. If you're feeling nostalgic for the 2000s for some reason, here's a chapter for you. There have been books penned which are solely devoted to this man, and here are his greatest hits:

### George W. Bush's political base:

*President George W. Bush at the 2000 Al Smith Dinner:* "This is an impressive crowd: the haves, and the have-mores. Some people call you the elite, I call you my base."

### Dick Cheney, on the deficit:

*In an interview with* 60 Minutes *on January 9, 2004, about Paul O'Neill's tell-all book on the Bush administration, when confronted about how the Iraq War would raise the deficit, Cheney responded:* "Reagan proved that deficits don't matter. We won the mid-term elections, this is our due."

### George W. Bush, on the White House:

*When asked what the White House was like by a student in East London, he told him:* "It is white." (September 13, 2004)

### Rebuilding his friend's house:

*While touring the Gulf Coast in the aftermath of Katrina, Bush joked:* "We've got a lot of rebuilding to do. . . . The good news is—and it's hard for some to see it now—that out of this chaos is going to come a fantastic Gulf Coast, like it was before. Out of the rubbles of Trent Lott's house—he's lost his entire house—there's going to be a fantastic house. And I'm looking forward to sitting on the porch." *(Mobile, Alabama, September 2, 2005)*

### This quote needs no introduction:

*In Bentonville, Arkansas, November 6, 2000, he uttered one of his most famous lines:* "They misunderestimated me."

### Neither does this one:

*George W. Bush, in La Crosse, Wisconsin:* "Families is where our nation finds hope. Where our wings take dream." *(October 8, 2000)*

### Donald Rumsfeld's unknown unknowns:

*Speaking at the United Nations, February 12, 2002:* "Reports that say something hasn't happened are always interesting to me, because as we know, there are known knowns; there are things we know we know. We also know there are known unknowns; that is to say we know there are some things we do not know. But there are also unknown unknowns—the ones we don't know we don't know."

### President George W. Bush, on anticipation:

*On* Good Morning America, *September 1, 2005, six days after repeated warnings from experts about the scope of damage expected from Hurricane Katrina, Bush explained:* "I don't think anybody anticipated the breach of the levees."

### George W. Bush, on important questions:

"I think anybody who doesn't think I'm smart enough to handle this job is underestimating." *(US News & World Report, April 3, 2008)*

---

*In Florence, South Carolina, speaking about the No Child Left Behind Act, November 11, 2000:* "Rarely is the question asked, 'Is our children learning?'"

### On the economy:

*Bush flubbed in his campaign speech in Rochester, New York, January 7, 2000:* "If the terriers and barriffs . . . are torn down, this economy will grow."

### George W. Bush, on important issues:

*While discussing malpractice lawsuit reforms, September 6, 2004:* "Too many ob-gyns aren't able to practice their love with women across this country."

---

*From his speech to the Nashua Chamber of Commerce in New Hampshire, January 27, 2000:* "If you're a single mother with two children—which is the toughest job in America, as far as I'm concerned—you're working hard to put food on your family."

### Attorney General Alberto Gonzalez, on eighteenth-/nineteenth-century electronic surveillance:

*Testifying before Congress in 2006, Gonzales tried to explain the history of electronic surveillance:* "President Washington, President Lincoln, President Wilson, President Roosevelt have all authorized electronic surveillance on a far broader scale." *(There was obviously no electronic surveillance back when these guys were president—except perhaps listening into telephone calls for some.)*

### George W. Bush, congratulating the FEMA director after Katrina:

"Brownie, you're doing a heck of a job." *(September 2, 2005)*

### First Lady Laura Bush, on hurricane names:

*While speaking to children and parents in South Haven, Mississippi, twice slipping up on the name of Hurricane Katrina, September 8, 2005:* "I also want to encourage anybody who was affected by Hurricane Corina to make sure their children are in school."

### George W. Bush, on shootings:

*In Philadelphia, Pennsylvania, May 14, 2001:* "For every fatal shooting, there were roughly three nonfatal shootings. And, folks, this is unacceptable in America. It's just unacceptable, and we're going to do something about it."

### This answer from Bush:

*On CNN, August 1, 2009, after being asked if the war in Iraq and the rise of terrorism are signs of the apocalypse:* "Hmmm, uhh, hah . . . ummm . . . I, the answer is . . . I haven't really thought of it that way, heh, heh. Heh. Here's how I think of it. Ummm . . . heh heh. First I've heard of that, by the way, I, ah . . . uhh . . . the, uhh . . . I, I guess I'm more of a practical fella. Uhh. I vowed after September the 11th that I would do everything I could to protect the American people. And, uhh . . . my attitude, of course, was affected by the attacks. Ha ha . . . ummm. Let me see . . . I knew we were at a war. I knew that the enemy, obviously, had to be sophisticated, and lethal, to fly hijacked airplanes, uhh, into . . . facilities that would, we would, killing thousands of people, innocent people, doin' nothing, just sittin' there goin' to work."

### Homeland Security Secretary Michael Chertoff, responding to reports that thousands in New Orleans were without food and water in FEMA camps:

"I have not heard a report of thousands of people in the convention center who don't have food and water." *(On NPR's* All Things Considered, *September 1, 2005)*

### Former President George W. Bush, on Katrina rumors:

*In an interview with CNN's Larry King, September 5, 2005, about the National Guard being deployed during Katrina:* "You know I talked to Haley Barbour, the governor of Mississippi yesterday because some people were saying, 'Well, if you hadn't sent your National Guard to Iraq, we here in Mississippi would be better off.' He told me, 'I've been out in the field every single day, hour, for four days and no one, not one single mention of the word Iraq.' Now where does that come from? Where does that story come from if the governor is not picking up one word about it? I don't know. I can use my imagination."

### On Hurricane Katrina:

*Rep. Richard Baker (R-LA) to lobbyists, as quoted in the* Wall Street Journal *in September 2005:* "We finally cleaned up public housing in New Orleans. We couldn't do it, but God did."

---

*At a news conference, Homeland Security Secretary Michael Chertoff exclaimed:* "Louisiana is a city that is largely underwater." *(September 3, 2005. I bet he meant to say "state.")*

---

*FEMA Director Michael Brown, August 28, 2005:* "FEMA is not going to hesitate at all in this storm. We are not going to sit back and make this a bureaucratic process. We are going to move fast, we are going to move quick, and we are going to do whatever it takes to help disaster victims." *(Four days after the quote above, Brown said to ABC's Ted Koppel:* "We just learned of the convention center—we being the federal government—today.")

---

*Ron Paul, in September 2003, calling for the end of FEMA just as Hurricane Irene was slamming the east coast, costing many lives and a lot of damage:* "A state can decide. We don't need somebody in Washington. I live on the gulf coast, we deal with hurricanes all the time. The local people rebuild the city. Built a sea wall and they survived without FEMA. We should be like 1900, we should be like 1940, 1950, 1960."

---

*House Speaker Dennis Hastert (R-IL), August 31, 2005, about repairing New Orleans after Katrina:* "It makes no sense to spend billions of dollars to rebuild a city that's seven feet under sea level. . . . It looks like a lot of that place could be bulldozed."

---

*In various leaked emails to colleagues and friends in the immediate aftermath of Hurricane Katrina, it appears that director Michael Brown was very concerned with his wardrobe:* "If you'll look at my lovely FEMA attire you'll really vomit. I am a fashion god. . . . Anything specific I need to do or tweak? Do you know of anyone who dog-sits? . . . Can I quit now? Can I come home? I'm trapped now, please rescue me."

---

*New Orleans Mayor Ray Nagin, when asked by NBC's Tim Russert on September 11, 2005, why he didn't follow the city's evacuation plan to use buses to get residents out during Katrina:* "You know, Tim, that's one of the things that will be debated."

---

*GOP strategist Jack Burkman, on MSNBC's* Connected, *September 7, 2005:* "I understand there are 10,000 people dead. It's terrible. It's tragic. But in a democracy of 300 million people, over years and years and years, these things happen."

---

*Sen. David Vitter (R-LA), in a press briefing from Baton Rouge, August 30, 2005:* "We don't want to alarm everybody that, you know, New Orleans is filling up like a bowl. That's just not happening." *(It was.)*

### George W. Bush, on terrorism:

"I'm telling you there's an enemy that would like to attack America, Americans, again. There just is. That's the reality of the world. And I wish him all the very best." *(Washington, DC, January 12, 2009)*

### Secretary of State Colin Powell, on the WMDs not found in Iraq:

*Addressing the United Nations in 2003 on Iraqi weapons of mass destruction:* "Every statement I make today is backed up by sources, solid sources. These are not assertions. What we are giving you are facts and conclusions based on solid intelligence."

### On devastation levels:

*While surveying damage of Louisiana from* Air Force One *on August 31, 2005, George W. Bush turned to one of his aides and said:* "It's totally wiped out. It's devastating, it's got to be doubly devastating on the ground."

### On the damage in New Orleans after Katrina:

*In an interview with CNN on September 1, 2005, FEMA Director Michael Brown speculated about people stranded in their homes and implying they bore some responsibility:* "I don't make judgments about why people chose not to leave but, you know, there was a mandatory evacuation of New Orleans."

---

*After the evacuation plan was bungled, Dick Cheney asserted on September 10, 2005:* "There are a lot of lessons we want to learn out of this process in terms of what works. I think we are in fact on our way to getting on top of the whole Katrina exercise."

Sh*t Politicians Say

### George W. Bush, on hearing voices:

"People say, well, do you ever hear any other voices other than, like, a few people? Of course I do." *(Washington, DC, December 18, 2008)*

### I found this quote from George W. Bush, about the 2008 market crash:

*In an ABC News interview on December 1, 2008, about the market crash and recession, Bush discussed his role in the crash:* "You know, I'm the president during this period of time, but I think when the history of this period is written, people will realize a lot of the decisions that were made on Wall Street took place over a decade or so, before I arrived in president, during I arrived in president."

### George W. Bush, still looking for the Book of W:

"I've been in the Bible every day since I've been the president." *(Washington, DC, November 12, 2008. The* Book of W *has yet to be written.)*

### George W. Bush, on dancing:

*Speaking with the president of Liberia in Washington, DC, October 22, 2008:* "Yesterday, you made note of my—the lack of my talent when it came to dancing. But nevertheless, I want you to know I danced with joy. And no question Liberia has gone through very difficult times."

### On his wife's "involvement":

*Promoting PlayPumps International, which improves access to clean water in Africa, Washington DC, October 21, 2008:* "I want to share with you an interesting program—for two reasons, one, it's interesting, and two, my wife thought of it—or has actually been involved with it; she didn't think of it. But she thought of it for this speech."

### George W. Bush, on persecuting Wall Street crooks:

"Anyone engaging in illegal financial transactions will be caught and persecuted." *(Washington, DC, September 19, 2008)*

### George W. Bush, on wildlife:

"The only place on earth where crocodiles and alligators live side by side." *(*Time, *June 2001)*

––––––––––

"I know the human being and the fish can coexist peacefully." *(Speech in Saginaw, Michigan, September 29, 2000)*

### Bush, on Iran having nukes:

*Speaking to reporters in Washington, DC, July 2, 2008:* "Should the Iranian regime—do they have the sovereign right to have civilian nuclear power? So, like, if I were you, that's what I'd ask me. And the answer is, yes, they do."

### Bush, on US retaliation:

*In an interview with* The Nation, *February 9, 2004:* "In my judgment, when the United States says there will be serious consequences, and if there isn't serious consequences, it creates adverse consequences."

### George W. Bush, on not being a mermaid:

"I didn't grow up in the ocean—as a matter of fact—near the ocean—I grew up in the desert. Therefore, it was a pleasant contrast to see the ocean. And I particularly like it when I'm fishing." *(Washington, DC, September 26, 2008)*

**George W. Bush, about steep gas prices:**

"I think it was in the Rose Garden where I issued this brilliant statement: If I had a magic wand—but the president doesn't have a magic wand. You just can't say, 'low gas.'" *(Washington DC, July 15, 2008)*

**George W. Bush to Pope Benedict XVI:**

"Your eminence, you're looking good." *(Using the title for Catholic cardinals, rather than addressing him as "your holiness," Rome, June 13, 2008)*

———

Thank you, Your Holiness. Awesome speech." *(George W. Bush, to Pope Benedict, Washington, DC, April 15, 2008)*

**President George W. Bush, thinking Africa is a country (it's a frikkin' epidemic!):**

*After meeting with the leaders of the European Union, Gothenburg, Sweden, June 14, 2001.* "We spent a lot of time talking about Africa, as we should. Africa is a nation that suffers from incredible disease."

**George W. Bush, on international relations:**

"We've got a lot of relations with countries in our neighborhood." *(Kranj, Slovenia, June 10, 2008)*

**George Bush, on his legacy:**

"I'll be long gone before some smart person ever figures out what happened inside this Oval Office." *(George W. Bush, Washington, DC, May 12, 2008)*

**George W. Bush, on winning elections:**

"Let me start off by saying that in 2000 I said, 'Vote for me. I'm an agent of change.' In 2004, I said, 'I'm not interested in change— I want to continue as president.' Every candidate has got to say 'change.' That's what the American people expect." *(Washington, DC, March 5, 2008)*

### President George W. Bush, on the No Child Left Behind Act:

"As yesterday's positive report card shows, childrens do learn when standards are high and results are measured." *(September 26, 2007)*

### President George W. Bush, on being fooled:

"There's an old saying in Tennessee—I know it's in Texas, probably in Tennessee—that says, fool me once, shame on—shame on you. Fool me—you can't get fooled again." *(September 17, 2002)*

### President George W. Bush, on Chanukah:

"I couldn't imagine somebody like Osama bin Laden understanding the joy of Chanukah." *(December 2006)*

### George W. Bush, on gas prices:

"Wait a minute. What did you just say? You're predicting $4-a-gallon gas? . . . That's interesting. I hadn't heard that." *(Washington, DC, February 28, 2008)*

### On his plan for peace in the Middle East:

*George W. Bush, on how he can contribute to the Middle East peace process, at a press conference in Washington, DC, January 4, 2008*: "I can press when there needs to be pressed; I can hold hands when there needs to be—hold hands."

### George W. Bush, on attacks on Americans:

"Our enemies are innovative and resourceful, and so are we. They never stop thinking about new ways to harm our country and our people, and neither do we." *(August 5, 2004)*

　　　　　　　　　　　　　Sh*t Politicians Say

### On pollution:

*George W. Bush at his last G-8 Summit, July 10th, 2008, said while punching the air and grinning:* "Goodbye from the world's biggest polluter."

### On running the country:

*Bush, meeting with congressional leaders in Washington DC, December 18, 2000:* "If this were a dictatorship, it'd be a heck of a lot easier, just so long as I'm the dictator."

### He were president:

*George W. Bush, on* Sean Hannity, *February 16, 2016:* "I love America and I know we face enormous problems, but I know we can deal with them. I know we can handle them. I'm not an expert in a lot of things, but I'm pretty knowledgeable about what it take to be President, since 'I were one.' And he's got what it takes. He's got character, backbone, philosophy, vision, and he'd make a really good president."

### George W. Bush, bringing peaceful Iraqis to justice?:

"The ambassador and the general were briefing me on the—the vast majority of Iraqis want to live in a peaceful, free world. And we will find these people and we will bring them to justice." *(Washington, DC, October 27, 2003)*

### George W. Bush, on how he reads the news:

"I glance at the headlines just to kind of get a flavor for what's moving. I rarely read the stories, and get briefed by people who are probably read the news themselves." *(Washington, DC, September 21, 2003)*

### George W. Bush, on peace and security:

"Security is the essential roadblock to achieving the road map to peace." *(Washington, DC, July 25, 2003)*

### On going home:

*FEMA Director Michael Brown, on his plans after being relieved from his role managing Hurricane Katrina relief efforts:* "I'm going to go home and walk my dog and hug my wife, and maybe get a good Mexican meal and a stiff margarita and a full night's sleep." *(September 9, 2005)*

### When you want advice, don't ask the wrong father:

*When Bob Woodward interviewed George W. Bush for his 2004 book* Plan of Attack, *he asked whether W. asked George senior for advice about Iraq, considering Dad also had his conflicts with Saddam. George W. said no, that he would be:* ". . . the wrong father to appeal to for advice . . . there is a higher father that I appeal to . . . I was praying for strength to do the Lord's will." *(Wow, how many politicians can say they have God on speed dial?)*

# Chapter 14

# *Sh\*t Sarah Palin Says*

Here's another person I hate with a burning passion, only partly because she's a quitter. Not only do I think she is an incompetent moron (and would've been a disaster for the country if McCain were elected and died of a heart attack mid-office, anointing her as commander-in-chief), but she quits. I hate quitters. So including a smattering of her stupid sayings in the book was another joy of mine.

### On qualifications:

*Sarah Palin, Fox News interview with Sean Hannity, November 22, 2010, about the media:* "I want to help clean up the state that is so sorry today of journalism. And I have a communications degree."

### On Conservatism:

*Sarah Palin, endorsing Donald Trump, January 18, 2016:* "Donald Trump and his Trumpeteers, well, they're not conservative enough. My goodness gracious. What the heck would the establishment know about conservatism?"

### *Sarah Palin, on language (some all her own):*

"'Refudiate,' 'misunderestimate,' 'wee-wee'd up.' English is a living language. Shakespeare liked to coin new words too. Got to celebrate it!" *(Twitter, July 18, 2010)*

### Why Sarah Palin writes on the palm of her hand:

*At a Right to Life fund-raiser, May 2010:* "I didn't really had a good answer, as so often—is me. But then somebody sent me the other day, Isaiah 49:16, and you need to go home and look it up. Before you look it up, I'll tell you what it says though. It says, hey, if it was good enough for God, scribbling on the palm of his hand, it's good enough for me, for us. He says, in that passage, 'I wrote your name on the palm of my hand to remember you,' and I'm like, 'Okay, I'm in good company.'"

### Sarah Palin found the door to heaven:

*Sarah Palin, May 20, 2013, speculating on what happened to Flight 370 (a plane that went missing over the Indian Ocean) on Fox News:* "How do you know there's not a door to heaven in the sky between Malaysia and Vietnam?"

### On sports:

Sarah Palin, *July 3, 2009, part of her announcement that she was resigning as governor of Alaska:* "Let me go back to a comfortable analogy for me—sports . . . basketball. I use it because you're naive if you don't see the national full-court press picking away right now: A good point guard drives through a full court press, protecting the ball, keeping her eye on the basket . . . and she knows exactly when to pass the ball so that the team can WIN."

### I don't think that means what you think it means:

*In the wake of the Arizona shooting, Sarah Palin found herself having to defend her campaign that used fiery language and crosshairs. This is what she posted to her Facebook page on January 12, 2011:* "Especially within hours of a tragedy unfolding, journalists and pundits should not manufacture a blood libel that serves only to incite the very hatred and violence they purport to condemn. That is reprehensible." *(Note: "blood libel" typically refers historically to the alleged murder of Christian babies by Jews.)*

---

*Sarah Palin, on why she doesn't keep up with the news, said during a fund-raiser in Greensboro, North Carolina, on October 16, 2008:* "At those times on the campaign trail when sometimes it's easy to get a little bit discouraged, when, you know, when you happen to turn on the news when your campaign staffers will let you turn on the news . . . Usually they're like "Oh my gosh, don't watch. You're going to, you know, you're going to get depressed."

---

"As Putin rears his head and comes into the airspace of America, where do they go? It's Alaska. It's right over the border." *(Sarah Palin, CBS News, 2008)*

**Word salad from Sarah Palin at the Iowa Freedom Summit, January 24, 2015:**

"He who was the one, now, with tea-time on the mind . . . now, this is to forego a conclusion, right, it's to scare us off and convince us that a pantsuit can crush patriots?! It's kind of Orwellian, observing, how that rule works, that rule of Saul Alinsky's, no doubt."

---

"Things must change for our government. Look at it. It isn't too big to fail. It's too big to succeed! It's too big to succeed, so we can afford no retreads or nothing will change with the same people and same policies that got us into the status quo. Another Latin word, status quo, and it stands for, 'Man, the middle-class everyday Americans are really gettin' taken for a ride.' That's status quo, and GOP leaders, by the way, y'know the man can only ride ya when your back is bent. . . . So strengthen it. Then the man can't ride ya, America won't be taken for a ride, because so much is at stake and we can't afford politicians playing games like nothing more is at stake than, oh, maybe just the next standing of theirs in the next election." *(January 24, 2015)*

### Sarah Palin, on Paul Revere's Midnight Ride:

"He who warned, uh, the British that they weren't gonna be takin' away our arms, uh, by ringing those bells, and um, makin' sure as he's riding his horse through town to send those warning shots and bells that we were going to be sure and we were going to be free, and we were going to be armed." *(June 3, 2011)*

### Sarah Palin, sending cryptic messages on Twitter?:

*After Dr. Laura Schlessinger used the* N *word on air eleven times in five minutes (and subsequently apologized and retired early), Palin defended Schlessinger in a bizarre Twitter message, August 18, 2010:* "Dr. Laura: don't retreat . . . reload! (Steps aside bc her 1st Amend. rights ceased 2exist thx 2activists trying 2silence "isn't American, not fair")"

### On death panels:

"The America I know and love is not one in which my parents or my baby with Down syndrome will have to stand in front of Obama's 'death panel' so his bureaucrats can decide, based on a subjective judgment of their 'level of productivity in society,' whether they are worthy of health care. Such a system is downright evil." *(Facebook post, August 7, 2009)*

### Sarah Palin, for Donald:

*Endorsing Trump for president on January 19, 2016, and responding to his Republican critics:* "Our own GOP machine, the establishment, they who would assemble the political landscape, they're attacking their own front-runner."

### On vetting:

*Sarah Palin, KWHL's Bob and Mark Show in Anchorage, November 17, 2010:* "We know that Obama wasn't vetted through the campaign, and now, you know, some things are coming home to roost, if you will, which is inexperience, his associations, and that ultimately harms our republic when a candidate isn't, isn't vetted by the media, that cornerstone of our democracy." *(This coming from an inexperienced, not well-vetted VP nominee!)*

### Sarah Palin, on making America "great again" (endorsing Donald Trump, January 19, 2016. She was on a roll):

"Are you ready to make America great again? We all have a part in this. We all have a responsibility. Looking around at all of you, you hard-working Iowa families. You farm families, and teachers, and teamsters, and cops, and cooks. You rocking rollers. And holy rollers! All of you who work so hard. You full-time moms. You with the hands that rock the cradle."

---

"The self-made success of his [Trump's]—you know that he doesn't get his power, his high, off OPM, other people's money, like a lot of dopes in Washington do. They're addicted to OPM, where they take other people's money, and then their high is getting to redistribute it, right? [. . .] His power, his passion, is the fabric of America. And it's woven by work ethic and dreams and drive and faith in the Almighty, what a combination."

———————

"And he, who would negotiate deals, kind of with the skills of a community organizer maybe organizing a neighborhood tea, well, he deciding that, 'No, America would apologize as part of the deal,' as the enemy sends a message to the rest of the world that they capture and we kowtow, and we apologize, and then, we bend over and say, 'Thank you, enemy.'"

———————

"Where, in the private sector, you actually have to balance budgets in order to prioritize, to keep the main thing, the main thing, and he knows the main thing: a president is to keep us safe economically and militarily. He knows the main thing, and he knows how to lead the charge. So troops, hang in there, because help's on the way because he, better than anyone, isn't he known for being able to command, fire!"

———————

"Trump's candidacy, it has exposed not just that tragic ramifications of that betrayal of the transformation of our country, but too, he has exposed the complicity on both sides of the aisle that has enabled it, okay?"

———————

"He builds things, he builds big things, things that touch the sky."

———————

"Pro-life, pro-Second Amendment, strict constitutionality. Those things that are unifying values from big cities to tiny towns, from big mountain states and the Big Apple, to the big, beautiful heartland that's in between."

---

"Calling jihad on each other's heads."

### On NOW (National Organization for Women):

*Interview with Greta Van Susteren, March 24, 2011, responding to feminist group NOW coming to her defense:* "I need NOW's defense like a fish needs a bicycle. I don't want them to defend me." *(Note: a slogan from NOW was "a woman needs a man like a fish needs a bicycle.")*

### Sarah Palin, on the Islamic community center that was planned near Ground Zero:

*She posted this to Twitter, July 18, 2010:* "Ground Zero Mosque supporters: doesn't it stab you in the heart, as it does ours throughout the heartland? Peaceful Muslims, pls refudiate." *(Then she quickly removed it after being ridiculed for inventing the word "refudiate.")*

### On hockey moms:

*McCain campaign rally, September 6, 2008:* "I love those hockey moms. You know what they say the difference between a hockey mom and a pit bull is? Lipstick."

### Assuring us she reads all the newspapers (from "Sarah Palin Interviews with Katie Couric" series, September 2008):

COURIC: And when it comes to establishing your world view, I was curious, what newspapers and magazines did you regularly read before you were tapped for this—to stay informed and to understand the world?

PALIN: I've read most of them again with a great appreciation for the press, for the media . . .

COURIC: But what ones specifically? I'm curious.

PALIN: Um, all of them, any of them that have been in front of me over all these years.

COURIC: Can you name any of them?

PALIN: I have a vast variety of sources where we get our news.

### Sarah Palin on vice president duties:

*During an interview with KUSA, October 21, 2008, Palin was asked by a student what the vice president does:* "That's something that Piper would ask me! . . . They're in charge of the US Senate so if they want to they can really get in there with the senators and make a lot of good policy changes that will make life better for Brandon and his family and his classroom."

### Sarah Palin, on foreign country locations:

*On CBS News, 2008:* "Our neighbors are foreign countries. They are in the state that I am the executive of."

### Sarah Palin, on Obama:

*Endorsing Donald Trump for president, January 20, 2016:* "President Obama will be able to look up, and there, over his head, he'll be able to see that shining, towering, Trump tower."

———

*Speaking at a Tea Party rally September 9, 2015, about the Iran Nuclear Deal:* "Only in an Orwellian [Barack] Obama world full of sprinkly fairy dust broken from atop his unicorn as he's peeking through a really pretty pink kaleidoscope would he ever see victory or safety for America or Israel in this treaty. This treaty will not bring peace. You don't reward terrorism. You kill it!"

*From her book* Going Rogue, *2009:*

"I always remind people from outside our state that there's plenty of room for all Alaska's animals—right next to the mashed potatoes."

———

"There were times (during my early campaigns) when I thought, 'You know what I could really use? A wife.'"

———

"Bear hunting? Come on up and we'll fix you up, you betcha. Just be sure you bring some hunting buddies with you, preferably fat ones who can't run as fast as you."

———

"If any vegans came over for dinner, I could whip them up a salad, then explain my philosophy on being a carnivore: If God had not intended for us to eat animals, how come He made them out of meat?"

OUR NEIGHBORS ARE FOREIGN COUNTRIES

# Chapter 15

## *Just Plain Weird Sh\*t*

"If you don't mind smelling like peanut butter for two or three days, peanut butter is darn good shaving cream."

—Barry Goldwater, former senator from Arizona

This is the stuff that is just plain weird. From Martian negotiations to pizza, this is stuff that makes you wonder whether your favorite candidate, local congressman, or president is on drugs and if so, what kind. I couldn't find a place for them, but now they're in the perfect place.

### Oh, boy! National Peach Month!:

*Former senate majority leader (and former presidential candidate) Bob Dole, on government efficiency, 1982:* "It may come as a shock to you who live out in the real world, but occasionally we do something up here. Not often, I admit, but sometimes. For example, I think the House has passed National Peach Month so far this year and we expect to act on it soon."

### Ted Cruz, on Chuck Norris:

*At a town hall meeting in North Texas, August 22, 2013:* "And let me tell you, Chuck Norris wears Jim DeMint pajamas."

### Manly pizza:

*In an interview with* GQ *magazine in 2011, Herman Cain, CEO of Godfather's Pizza and former presidential nominee, discusses pizza toppings:* "The more toppings a man has on his pizza, I believe the more manly he is. A manly man don't want it piled high with vegetables! He would call that a sissy pizza."

### Mitt Romney, on breakfast:

*At Blake's Creamery in New Hampshire, June 14, 2011:* "I saw the young man over there with eggs Benedict, with hollandaise sauce. And I was going to suggest to you that you serve your eggs with hollandaise sauce in hubcaps. Because there's no plates like chrome for the hollandaise."

### Joni Ernst (R-IA), on farm life:

*From her campaign ad, March 24, 2014:* "I grew up castrating hogs on an Iowa farm, so when I come to Washington, I'll know how to cut pork."

### Joe Biden, on the film Deliverance:

"After those guys tied that one guy to the tree and raped him, man-raped him in the film, why didn't the guy go to the sheriff? . . . They don't want to get raped again by the system." *(May 1, 2013)*

### On finding attractive women:

*Former senator and presidential candidate Gary Hart, explaining a photo of Donna Rice on his lap, June 1987:* "The attractive lady whom I had only recently been introduced to dropped into my lap. . . . I chose not to dump her off."

### On the virtues of volleyball:

*Boris Johnson, mayor of London, checks in with this, about the women's Olympic volleyball team, July 30, 2012:* "As I write these words there are semi-naked women playing beach volleyball in the middle of the horse guards parade immortalized by Canaletto. They are glistening like wet otters and the water is splashing off the brims of the spectators' sou'westers."

### Whoops:

"For seven and a half years I've worked alongside President Reagan. We've had triumphs. Made some mistakes. We've had some sex . . . uh . . . setbacks." *(George H. W. Bush. 1988)*

### That sounds wrong:

*Rick Santorum at the Iowa State Convention, June 16, 2014:* "Look, I understand why campaigns and all of you want to go out and just bang the president. It's fun."

### Congressmen sext, too:

*Stephen Cohen text message, February 13, 2012:* "nice to know you were watchin SOTU [State of the Union]. Happy Valentines beautiful girl. ilu"

———————

*Bob Filner, voicemail, August 2012:* "Eldonna, hi, it's your newly favorite congressman, Bob Filner. You know, the one who fell in love with you at your last speech. Hey, I'm just wondering, are you gonna to be in town for a couple days or are you going back, uh, cuz I don't want to wait 'til you come back to have dinner with you."

### Gee, brain, what are we gonna do tonight?:

"American scientific companies are cross-breeding humans and animals and coming up with mice with fully functioning human brains." *(Christine O'Donnell, on* Bill O'Reilly, *2007)*

### Measuring trees:

*Mitt Romney, campaigning in Michigan, February 2012:* "I love this state. The trees are the right height."

### Seriously, what were YOU smoking?:

*George Bush Sr., speaking about Al Gore during the 1992 presidential campaign to the* Spiderman *theme song:* "Ozone Man, Ozone. He's crazy, way out, far out, man."

### Do you want squirrel meat with that?:

"When we were in college we used to take a popcorn popper—because that was the only thing they would let us have in the dorms—and fry squirrels in the popcorn popper." *(Mike Huckabee, January 18, 2008, in an interview on MSNBC's* Morning Joe*)*

### That's nice:

*Rob Ford (Independent, Canada), Mayor of Toronto, on* Coffee Run *web series, July 2015:* "I have a lot of Italian friends and they have espressos."

### Jefferson Parish Sheriff Newell Normand, on how Jim Jones died:

*Speaking at a Crime Commission Awards Luncheon, February 2016:* "What a mess. Bobby Jindal was a better cult leader than Jim Jones. We drank the elixir for eight years. We remained in a conscious state; we walked to the edge of the cliff, and he watched. And guess what? Unlike Jim Jones, he did not swallow the poison.

Sh*t Politicians Say

What a shame." *(Jim Jones died from a gunshot wound that was either self-inflicted, or one of his lackeys shot him. Good hyperbole, but wrong. Love your vitriol, though, dude.)*

### On John Wayne Gacy:

*Michele Bachmann, at a campaign stop in Waterloo, Iowa, June 27, 2011:* "What I want them to know is just like John Wayne was from Waterloo, Iowa, that's the spirit that I have too. It's really about not being ashamed of America. It's embracing America." *(Note: the John Wayne from Waterloo, Iowa, was serial killer John Wayne Gacy, not the movie actor, who was from Winterset.)*

# Chapter 16

## *Last But Not Least: Sh\*t I've Said*

"The people in Washington could not be more surprised if Fidel Castro came loping across the Midwestern prairie on the back of a Hippopotamus."

> —Dan Rather, in a flustered election-night report of my election.

And finally, here's some of the ridiculous shit I have said over the years. I don't think some of it is ridiculous, of course, but some of it I drew a lot of flack for. Here's some explanation, which I don't owe you, but here it is:

### I hate it when funerals are politicized:

*After leaving a memorial ceremony for Democratic US Senator Paul Wellstone, October 30, 2002:* "I feel used. I feel violated and duped over the fact that that turned into nothing more than a political rally."

### On volunteering:

*Quoted in the* Army Times, *September 6, 2004:* "The current use of the National Guard is wrong. . . . These are men who did not sign up to go occupy foreign nations."

### On sex work:

*From my interview in* Playboy, *which critics fried me for (I still stand by it):* "We call our country home of the brave and land of

199

the free, but it's not. We give a false portrayal of freedom. We're not free—if we were, we'd allow people their freedom. Prohibiting something doesn't make it go away. Prostitution is criminal, and bad things happen because it's run illegally by dirt-bags who are criminals. If it's legal, then the girls could have health checks, unions, benefits, anything any other worker gets, and it would be far better." *(November 1999)*

## On religion:

*Again, from my interview in* Playboy*:* "Organized religion is a sham and a crutch for weak-minded people who need strength in numbers. It tells people to go out and stick their noses in other people's business. I live by the golden rule: Treat others as you'd want them to treat you. The religious right wants to tell people how to live."

## On fitness:

"Every fat person says it's not their fault, that they have gland trouble. You know which gland? The saliva gland. They can't push away from the table."

## On bras:

"If I could be reincarnated as a fabric, I would come back as a 38 double-D bra."

## On speaking my mind:

*Me, summing up the interview quotes above on NBC's* Meet the Press*, October 3, 1999:* "I speak my mind. If it offends some people, well, there's not much I can do about that. But I'm going to be honest. I'm going to continue to speak my mind, and that's who I am. . . ."

---

Sh*t Politicians Say

*Speaking in a news conference to reporters, February 23, 2001, where a few were wearing the "Official Jackal" security passes that I had issued:* "Congratulations, you have a sense of humor. And to those who didn't: Go stick your head in the mud."

### On meeting the Dalai Lama:

*On what I spoke about in my meeting with Tenzin Gyatso, the 14th Dalai Lama, on May 9, 2001, a scene in that film has the character played by Bill Murray telling a story about having caddied for the Dalai Lama. If you haven't seen this movie, go watch it. It's hilarious:* "I asked him the most important question that I think you could ask—if he had ever seen *Caddyshack*."

### Why I don't legislate patriotism or prayer:

*On May 22, 2002, explaining my veto of a bill [HF 2598\*/SF 2411/CII 391] requiring public school students to recite the Pledge of Allegiance at least once a week:* "I believe patriotism comes from the heart. Patriotism is voluntary. It is a feeling of loyalty and allegiance that is the result of knowledge and belief. A patriot shows their patriotism through their actions, by their choice. Chapter 391 is not about choice. In Chapter 391, the State mandates patriotic actions and displays. Our government should not dictate actions. The United States of America exists because people wanted to be free to choose. All of us should have free choice when it comes to patriotic displays . . . a government wisely acting within its bounds will earn loyalty and respect from its citizens. A government dare not demand the same. There is much more to being a patriot and a citizen than reciting the pledge or raising a flag. Patriots serve. Patriots vote. Patriots attend meetings in their community. Patriots pay attention to the actions of government and speak out when needed.

Patriots teach their children about our history, our precious democracy and about citizenship. Being an active, engaged citizen means being a patriotic American every day. No law will make a citizen a patriot."

———

*Explaining my refusal to sign a "National Day of Prayer" proclamation, May 6, 1999:* "I believe in the separation of church and state. . . . We all have our own religious beliefs. There are people out there who are atheists, who don't believe at all. . . . They are all citizens of Minnesota and I have to respect that.

## On torture:

"If waterboarding is okay, then why don't we let our police do it to criminals so they can find out what they know? Because it's against the law. If we're not going to be a country that stands for the rule of law, when it's convenient or inconvenient, then what DO we stand for." *(me, in an interview on* The View, *May 19, 2009)*

———

"Enhanced interrogation is Dick Cheney changing a word. Dick Cheney comes up with a new word to cover his ass!" *(me, same interview, May 19, 2009)*

———

"It's a good thing I'm not the president, because I would prosecute everybody who was involved in that torture, I would prosecute the people who did it, I would prosecute the people who ordered it and they would all go to jail! Because torture is against the law!"

———

*From* Larry King Live, *May 11, 2009:* "You give me a water board, Dick Cheney, and one hour, and I'll have him confess to the Sharon Tate murders."

---

"It's convenient how everyone who supports waterboarding and torture, or 'enhanced interrogation techniques' as they like to call it, have never experienced it themselves. Yet everyone who has, myself included, are firmly against it." *(as a military veteran)*

### On patriotism:

"If you're patriotic, stand up for the Bill of Rights because once they strip your rights from you, you will pay hell to get them back. You will, and we're in the process of it right now."

### On wrestling:

"Wrestling is ballet with violence."
"In wrestling, my mustache made me look more like a villain. A good mustache can give you the look of the devil."
"Did I die?" *(me, on the number of roses that were sent to me after my November 3 victory)*

### On taxes:

"Remember that government doesn't earn one single dollar it spends. In order for you to get money from the government, that money must first be taken from somebody else."

---

"I don't believe we need the government's help as much as some think we do. That belief sets me apart from the Democrats, since their way of dealing with everything is to tax and spend."

### On displays of patriotism:

"All of us should have free choice when it comes to patriotic displays . . . a government wisely acting within its bounds will earn loyalty and respect from its citizens. A government dare not demand the same."

### On airport trips:

"I have metal in my body, so every time I go to an airport, the metal detector goes off."

### On the government:

"Government works less efficiently when it begins to grow out of control and takes on more and more of the responsibilities that belong to the citizens."

———————

"Love is by far bigger than the government can ever be."

———————

"I love my country, not my government."

### On immigration:

"If you want to stop illegal immigration, you have to make it so that—so that the people that hire the illegal immigrants will not be in a position to hire them."

### On voting:

"Don't vote for a Democrat or Republican, I have never voted for one in my life and I never will." *(I was making a point that a voter should consider the person, not the party!)*

———————

"I have an idea about voting, how about on every ballot we include "None of the above." People may laugh at that, but what that is, it is a vote of no confidence in your government, and I'm willing to bet that in some elections, 'None of the Above' would win. Imagine if you won the election but lost to 'None of the Above.' Wouldn't that make you rethink your positions?"

### On abortion:

"I don't support abortion. I could never participate in one. But I think it would be a mistake to make them illegal again."

### On the FBI watchlist:

"Go to the Internet and go to the FBI website and go to their international list of top ten terrorists. You will see Bin Laden there, bring his name up and his picture. Amazingly, all the charges: the embassy of '98 and this other stuff is all listed. But, ironically nothing on 9/11. NOTHING! Now when the FBI was pressed as to why 9/11 wasn't included, their response was "We don't have enough evidence." Now, people, if you're like me that is extremely disturbing; we've fought two wars, we've changed our entire foreign policy and we've had the PATRIOT act put on us, all, supposedly, because of Osama Bin Laden!"

### On hunting:

In a pre-hunting interview with television reporters: "We're going to give the press a ten-minute head start, then that's what we're going to hunt."

### On guns:

*During a pre-election radio interview on the crime issue:* "Being able to put two rounds into the same hole from 25 meters! That's gun control."

### On pot:

*In a pre-election discussion on the decriminalization of marijuana:* "Anyway, I've done way more stupid things on alcohol than I have on pot."

### On roads:

"Whoever designed the streets must have been drunk. . . . I think it was those Irish guys." (Late Night with David Letterman*)*

### On the New World Order (a lot of this is sad, but true, and someone has to say it):

"We're in a world where common sense is considered radical."
"When I take my philosophy and I look at the borders, and I go, you know, they're all manmade. We're all human beings on this planet, why do we have to have paperwork to travel around on it?" *(*Evolution of the New World Order *podcast, November 26, 2014)*

### And lastly, on speaking my mind:

"I speak my mind. If it offends some people, well, there's not much I can do about that. But I'm going to be honest. I'm going to continue to speak my mind, and that's who I am."

# *Epilogue*

So here we are, at the end of the line. If you're like me, these quotes made you laugh, scratch your head, or even got you really, really angry. And I don't blame you, as politicians over the years really have certainly said their fair share of ignorant, inconsiderate, silly, and just plain stupid shit. And I bet with little effort, we could put together for your reading pleasure a *Volume Two*.

Don't kill me for saying this, but sometimes I have even felt sorry for these dopes. It's not easy being a politician in today's world of social media, sound bites, smart phone cameras, and the instant news cycle. Everything you say can and will be scrutinized and analyzed, the second after you say it, so don't put your foot in your mouth. And if you're outta line with the information you broadcast, people will throw it back in your face and call you out on it. It happened to me frequently when I was in the governor's office, and things are even worse now for politicos. Today, a politician better make pretty darn sure they've got their facts straight and the cojones to speak the truth, from the heart—or they might find themselves lambasted on Twitter and Facebook, CNN and Meet the Press . . . not to mention in books like this.

Peace!

## About the Author/Compiler

**JESSE VENTURA** is the former Independent governor of Minnesota. He is also a former US Navy frogman, a professional wrestler, a movie actor, a visiting fellow at Harvard Kennedy School of Government, and the *New York Times* bestselling author of seven books, including *American Conspiracies, 63 Documents the Government Doesn't Want You to Read*, and *Don't Start the Revolution Without Me*. He was the host and executive producer of truTV's *Conspiracy Theory with Jesse Ventura* as well as the host of the political show *Off the Grid*, which aired on RT America and online at Ora.tv. He has a reputation as a rebel and a freethinker; he also has no qualms about questioning authority. He spends half the year in Baja, Mexico, and the other half in his home state of Minnesota.